WHAT EVERY
CHRISTIAN
OUGHT TO KNOW

WHAT EVERY
CHRISTIAN
OUGHT TO KNOW

ESSENTIAL TRUTHS FOR GROWING YOUR FAITH

ADRIAN ROGERS

BROADMAN
& HOLMAN
PUBLISHERS

NASHVILLE, TENNESSEE

Ten-Digit ISBN: 0–8054–2692–2
Thirteen-Digit ISBN: 978–0–8054–2692–2

Published by Broadman & Holman Publishers
Nashville, Tennessee

Dewey Decimal Classification: 230
Subject Heading: CHRISTIAN DOCTRINE

Unless otherwise noted Scripture quotations are from the New
King James Version, copyright © 1979, 1980, 1982, Thomas
Nelson, Inc., Publishers. Scripture quotations marked KJV are from
the King James Version. Scripture quotations marked NASB are
from the New American Standard Bible, © the Lockman
Foundation, 1960, 1962, 1963, 1968, 1971, 1972, 1973, 1975,
1977; used by permission.

8 9 10 10 09 08 07 06

CONTENTS

WHAT YOU DON'T KNOW CAN HURT YOU

Wiped Out!

The waves were enormous, much bigger than those in my native state of Florida. We were in Maui, Hawaii, and I was excited. I love to bodysurf. Catch a wave just right, and you can ride without a board all the way to the beach.

I worked my way out to where the waves were breaking. I saw my wave building up. This would be a great ride. I knew I had to catch it just right. At the special moment I put my head down and gave a kick. The action really began.

The monster wave didn't take me to the beach. It picked me up like a rag doll and "body slammed" me on the ocean floor. The lights went out. I was numb. "Let me check. Can I move my legs, my arms?" Nothing was broken. I made my way carefully to the shore.

When I got back on solid ground, I turned to see the big sign posted:

NO BODYSURFING.
Serious Spinal Injury May Result.

There was the warning in plain sight, but I was saturated with ignorance. So much for the old proverb, *What you don't know can't hurt you.*

Education is costly, but ignorance may be devastating. There are some basic truths that every Christian ought to know. Many founder in a sea of moral relativism and vague religious opinions. Some may be body slammed, like I was, because they do not know.

Our society boasts about pluralism (there is room for every idea), but really practices syncretism by blending all religious thought into a bland mixture of spiritual pablum. Americans love to prate about values but are quickly intimidated when the question is asked, "Whose values?" It is more morality by majority than biblical virtues.

Some speak of education as the answer to most everything, and yet the more we know, the deeper we sink. We are "always learning and never able to come to the knowledge of the truth" (2 Tim. 3:7). Our generation has substituted facts for truth. We don't ask, "Is it true?" We just want to know, "Does it work?" Many Christians don't grow because they don't know. Facts are like a recipe, but truth is like a meal. Digest a truth and it will change your life.

"Buy the truth, and do not sell it" (Prov. 23:23).

- We must *prize* the truth.

    There is no way to be a happy, victorious Christian without a firm conviction based on foundational truth.
- We must *purchase* the truth.

    "Buy the truth." Salvation is free, but the quest for truth is costly. Yet while discipleship is costly, ignorance is far more costly. The quest for truth will cost precious time, discipline, and obedience, but it is worth it.

- We must *preserve* the truth.

  "Do not sell it." Some will tempt us to "sell out." Don't do it. Get a bulldog grip on the truth and never let go.

When the child of God
Loves the Word of God
And sees the Son of God,
He is changed by the Spirit of God
Into the image of God
For the glory of God
Because he has found the truth of God.

This book deals with the fundamental truth that *Every Christian Ought to Know.* It is written to be clear but not simplistic. It is for the new believer but also for those who seem bogged down in their Christian walk.

1

Every Christian Ought to Know
THE BIBLE IS THE WORD OF GOD

*All Scripture is given by inspiration of God, and is
profitable for doctrine, for reproof, for correction,
for instruction in righteousness, that the man of
God may be complete, thoroughly equipped for
every good work.*

2 TIMOTHY 3:16–17

The starting place in Christian growth is to have a firm conviction about the inspiration and authority of the Bible. In this chapter
I want to give some solid reasons to have this assurance. Believe me

when I tell you this is the starting place. You will not make solid progress without it.

Man Has Only Three Problems

While on an airplane, I was browsing the magazine selection looking for a newspaper. I met a man there who asked what kind of a newspaper I was looking for. I responded frankly that I was looking for a conservative newspaper.

He looked me up and down and said, "I'm looking for a liberal newspaper." He was wearing a dark pin-striped suit, and I asked him what he did. He responded that he was a lawyer and in return asked me what I did. I told him I was a Baptist preacher.

He was interested in what I read, and I told him that I read books, journals, and newspapers, but that I primarily read the Bible.

"You don't read any wider than that?" he asked.

"No, not really."

"Do you speak to people?"

"All the time."

He said, "Well then, how do you know what people's needs and what their problems are if you don't read any more widely than that?"

I said to this lawyer, "Man has only three problems: sin, sorrow, and death."

He said, "No, there are more problems than that."

I said, "All right, think about it and tell me a fourth problem."

He thought for a while, and then he said, "Man has only three problems."

Every other problem in the world is indeed just a subset of sin, sorrow, death, and the Bible is the *only book on earth* that has the answer to all three conditions. For this reason, it is important that you understand and have a rock-ribbed assurance that the Bible is the Word of God. It is not the Book of the Month; it is the Book of the Ages.

There Is a War on the Bible

The devil hates this book and would like to destroy it. Some despise the Bible; others just deny it; still others distort it and have warped, misused, and abused it. But I believe the greatest enemy of the Bible is the so-called Christian who simply ignores the Bible or disregards it. He gives only lip service to it.

"These hath God married and no man shall part:
Dust in the Bible and drought in the heart."

I have been serving Jesus for a long time, and the thing that keeps me going is truth and conviction. This conviction is not based on my feelings but on what I know is truth. Feelings come and go, but God's Word never wavers.

Why is this so important?

- Your salvation depends on understanding the gospel message of the Bible.
- Your assurance depends on resting in the truth of the Bible.
- Your spiritual growth depends on living by the principles of the Bible.
- Your power in witness depends on the confidence you have in the Word of God.

Therefore, you must be absolutely certain that the Bible is the Word of God. I want to give you some principles that have confirmed this certainty for me. Let me say that beyond these objective arguments, there is the sweet affirmation of the Holy Spirit to my heart concerning the Word of God. Jesus said, "My sheep hear My voice" (John 10:27). Think with me about the following confirmations of the inspiration of the Bible.

The Bible Is Shown to Be the Word of God Because of Its Scientific Accuracy

Scientific accuracy confirms the Bible as the Word of God. This first concept is the same one most often used to dispute the validity of the Bible by those who deny it. It is commonly assumed that, of course, there must be scientific errors in the Bible. Before you say that, however, make certain you know two things: *science* and *the Bible.* Most often those who claim scientific errors in the Bible do not clearly understand either subject. And those who do understand science must admit that it is in a continual state of flux, constantly changing. The accepted science of yesterday is not necessarily the science of today. It has been estimated that the library in the Louvre in Paris has three and a half miles of books on science. Most every one of them is obsolete.[1]

In 1861, the French Academy of Science wrote a pamphlet stating there were fifty-one incontrovertible scientific facts that proved the Bible not true. Today there is not a reputable scientist on Earth that believes one of those fifty-one so-called facts.[2] The point is, science is changing. God's Word does not change! Let me give a few examples:

The Earth Is Suspended in Space

One of the most fundamental scientific facts that you and I agree is true today is that our Earth is suspended in space. Ancient cultures did not always know this. The ancient Egyptians used to believe the Earth was supported by pillars. The Greeks believed the world was carried on the back of a giant whose name was Atlas. And the Hindus believed something even more ridiculous—that the Earth was resting on the backs of gigantic elephants. Then somebody said, "But wait a minute, what are the elephants standing on?" The answer was, "The elephants are standing on the back of a huge tortoise—a giant turtle." Then somebody asked, "What is the turtle resting on?" The answer, "Well, that turtle is on the back of a huge coiled serpent." And somebody said, "What is the serpent on?" The conclusion was that the serpent was swimming in a great cosmic sea. This was the science of that day!

When you and I pick up the Word of God, we do not find any such mythology. Job spoke of the Lord in chapter 26 verse 7: "He stretches out the north over the *empty* space; he hangs *the earth on nothing.*" Job is perhaps the oldest piece of literature known to man. How did Job know the Earth is suspended in space? Job could only know through divine inspiration. The Bible says in 2 Timothy 3:16 that "all Scripture is given by inspiration of God."

The Earth Is Round, Not Flat

We also take for granted that the Earth is round. Do we know this by natural observation? Not at all. You've seen pictures from outer space, and perhaps you have traveled around the world, so you take it for granted. But people didn't always know that the Earth was round. Remember that little saying from when you were in school, "In 1492, Columbus sailed the ocean blue"? They warned, "Columbus, you had better be careful; you might sail off the edge of the Earth."

Even as late as 1492, people did not know that the Earth is round. Yet Isaiah, in 750 BC, said, "It is He [God] who sits above the circle of the earth" (Isa. 40:22). The word for *circle* in the Hebrew is *chuwg,* which means "globe or sphere."[3]

How did Job know that God hung the Earth upon nothing? How did Isaiah know 750 years before Christ that the Earth is round? "Holy men of God spoke as they were moved by the Holy Spirit" (2 Pet. 1:21).

The Bible teaches that when Jesus comes again, it will be both daylight and dark. For example, "There will be two men in one bed: the one will be taken and the other will be left. Two men will be in the field; the one will be taken and the other left" (Luke 17:34–36). That seems contradictory. But while it will be light on one side of the globe, it will be dark on the other side when Jesus Christ comes again. Of course, all of this did not take the one who created the world by surprise; He knew all of it.

The Stars Cannot Be Counted

Here is another scientific fact relating to the science of the Bible. The stars in our galaxy are beyond ability to number. You and I would never be so foolish as to try to count the stars. But there was one man who laid down his pen, rubbed his eyes, and was weary because he had counted the stars, or so he thought. He was an astronomer 150 years before Christ. This man's name was Hipparchus, and he was the astronomer and scientist of his day. His study yielded 1,022 stars. He had counted the stars, he had made his chart—1,022 stars—and that was science.

His findings were considered accurate for 250 years, and then along came Ptolemy who began to count the stars and said, "Did

Hipparchus say there are 1,022 stars? How absurd—there are 1,056 stars." His count had upgraded the science of the day for a while.

About thirteen hundred years later, a young medical student named Galileo invented his first crude telescope, turned it up to the heavens, and looked beyond those stars that could be seen with the naked eye. There were more stars—and more stars—and hundreds and thousands and millions and billions and hundreds of billions of stars on and on and on! No fool would ever dare try to count the stars.

A while back I was reading in a scientific journal that scientists were trying to help us to understand the size of our universe. The journal stated that there are more suns like our sun in the known universe than there are grains of sand on all the seashores of the Earth.

I'm from West Palm Beach, Florida, and I can't even imagine counting the grains of sand just in a city block! And there are more suns in our universe than there are grains of sand on all of the seashores of the Earth! Think again of Hipparchus—one, two, three—1,022 stars! He could have saved some time had he turned to the Word of God. Jeremiah 33:22 states, "The host of heaven cannot be numbered."

Job says the Earth is floating in space. Isaiah says it is a globe. Jeremiah says you can't count the number of the stars.

The Blood Circulates through the Body

Let's move away from the area of astronomy and think about human anatomy and physiology. You and I take for granted that our blood is flowing in our body and is, what some have called, "a red river of life." It was not, however, until the year 1628 that William

Harvey, a medical doctor, discovered that the blood circulates throughout the body.

In college I took a course in human anatomy and physiology, and I learned all of the things the blood does. It carries fuel to the cells, carries oxygen to burn that fuel, carries away waste, fights disease, and maintains a constant temperature in the body. This is only recent knowledge, though. In the "olden days" when someone got sick, the comment would often be made, "He has bad blood." People thought they needed to get rid of some of that bad blood, so they would bleed these people. Can you imagine taking a person who is sick and draining his blood?

A barber pole looks like a piece of peppermint candy but was meant to represent a bandage. Often they would take sick people to the barber who would bleed them in order to make them well. Sometimes they would put leeches on them to take the blood out of them.

A little known fact is how George Washington, the father of our country, died. He was sick so the physicians bled him. When he didn't get well, they bled him again. He didn't get well, so they bled him a third time. They bled him to death! Could it be that ever since that time the politicians have been bleeding us to death to get even? Hmmm!

Today they might have given him a blood transfusion. The Bible tells us in Leviticus 17:14: "For it [blood] is the life of all flesh. Its blood sustains its life." The blood is the life of all flesh. How did Moses know of the life-giving property of the blood? Well, "all Scripture is given by inspiration of God." "Holy men of God spoke as they were moved by the Holy Spirit." The medical science in the Bible is truly wonderful.

Rattlesnake Fat and Worm's Blood

Dr. S. I. McMillen reports in his intriguing book *None of These Diseases* that archeologists have found a medical book called the Ebers Papyrus written by the Egyptians about fifteen hundred years before Christ, during the time of Moses.[4] The Egyptians were clever and skilled, yet they had some foolish ideas. Let me give you some of the medical knowledge that was in the Ebers Papyrus. I don't suggest you follow this advice.

For example, if you want to prevent your hair from turning gray, you can anoint it with the blood of a black cat that has been boiled in oil or with the fat of a rattlesnake. Or, if you want to keep your hair from falling out, take six fats, namely those of the horse, the hippopotamus, the crocodile, the cat, the snake, and the ibex. And if you want to strengthen your hair, anoint it with the tooth of a donkey crushed in honey.

If you have a splinter embedded under your skin, here is the recommended medicine—worm's blood and donkey dung. Can you imagine the tetanus spores that would be in donkey dung? Other kinds of drugs they used were lizard's blood, pig's teeth, rotten meat, moisture from pig's ears, and excreta from humans, animals, and even flies.

We are still trying to understand some of the things the Egyptians knew about embalming and a variety of other things. They were highly intelligent people. The Bible says that Moses was schooled in all the wisdom of the Egyptians. Moses went to the University of Egypt, and old Pharaoh paid his tuition. And I suppose he learned all of these things that were written in the Ebers Papyrus. Yet I am so glad that when I open the Bible I don't find any of these absurd treatments.

Answer to the Black Plague Found in Leviticus

In Europe during the fourteenth century, there was something called "the black plague." One out of four people died from the black plague. They didn't know what to do with it. They couldn't control it. They had no concept of microbiology like we have now. Do you know what finally brought the plague to an end? The Bible! Finally they turned to Scripture. Leviticus 13:46: "All the days he has the sore [the plague] he shall be unclean. He is unclean, and he shall dwell alone; his dwelling shall be outside the camp." They learned to quarantine from the Word of God.

Although I've mentioned several areas of science where the Bible has been vindicated, I have only touched the surface of the many medical and scientific truths contained in the Bible. Frankly, I'm glad the Bible and modern science don't always agree. Science changes. The Bible—never!

The Bible Is Shown to Be the Word of God Because of Its Historical Accuracy

The Bible is not primarily a science book. It is not written to tell us how the heavens go; it is written to tell us how to go to heaven. But when it speaks on science, it is accurate. And the Bible is not primarily a book of history. It is "His story," the story of God. But you would expect to find the history of the Bible to be accurate and to be true. However, as you might suspect, the Bible has been attacked because of its history.

In the late 1800s, the scholar Dr. S. R. Driver ridiculed the idea that Moses wrote what is called the Pentateuch, the first five books of the Bible—Genesis, Exodus, Leviticus, Numbers, and Deuteronomy.

Driver claimed, "In the time that Moses was supposed to have lived on the Earth, men didn't know how to write. So how could he have written the Pentateuch?"

So some scoffed at the Bible for a while until one day, in northern Egypt, a lady was spading her garden when she came across some clay tablets. They were called the Tel el-Amarna tablets and were tablets used for correspondence. They were written from people in Egypt to people in Palestine, or what we call today the Holy Land, centuries before Moses was born. Not only did they know how to write, but also they had a postal service that allowed them to send letters back and forth to one another. This proves that Moses did indeed have the capability to write the Pentateuch and also proves a learned man's opinion wrong.

In the book of Daniel is a story about the handwriting on the wall. King Belshazzar saw handwriting on the wall during a feast he made for a thousand of his lords and ladies. The gruesome handwriting told him he was weighed in the balances and found wanting. Do you remember the story? Well, scholars would laugh at that and say, "It's a fabrication. That never happened because we have the records of the ancient Babylonians, and we know that Belshazzar was not the last king of Babylon. The last king of Babylon was named Nabonitus. Obviously this would appear to be just some pious fraud, some story that somebody made up."

But one day the spade of an archeologist uncovered a cylinder, and sure enough, the name on it was Belshazzar. More records were found that showed the historians were right when they said that Nabonitus was the last king of Babylon, but they were wrong when they said that Belshazzar was not the last king of Babylon. Nabonitus and Belshazzar were father and son and had ruled together, making them both kings at the same time! Nabonitus was a big game hunter, among other things, and was often gone, leaving Belshazzar in charge. Remember what the king said to Daniel in Daniel 5:16 concerning the handwriting on the wall, "If you can read the writing and make known to me its interpretation you shall be clothed with purple and have a chain of gold around your neck, and shall be the *third* ruler in the kingdom." It makes sense now that we understand there were already two kings simultaneously.

Now what would have happened had they not found the cylinder with Belshazzar's name on it? Would the Bible be any less the Word of God? Just give people time, and maybe one day they'll catch up with the Bible. If a historian or a scientist has a good word to say about the Bible, it shouldn't give you any more faith in the Bible, just a little more faith in the scientist or the historian. The Bible has and will stand the test of time.

The Bible Is Shown to Be the Word of God Because of Its Wonderful Unity

Let me give you a third reason we can know the Bible is the Word of God. It is the wonderful unity of the Bible: one book, Genesis through Revelation, but it is also sixty-six books—thirty-nine books in the Old Testament and twenty-seven books in the New Testament. It is a compilation of books written by at least forty authors, and perhaps more. These people lived in a period of time that would span at least sixteen hundred years. They lived in about thirteen different countries and on three different continents.

Think about this. They came from all backgrounds: some were shepherds, and some were kings; some were soldiers, and others were princes; some were fishermen; some were scholars; some were historians; some were professional men, and some were common laborers. And the Bible is written in different styles and in at least three different languages. But when you bring all that together, it makes one book that has one story beginning with Genesis and going through Revelation.

- The Bible has one theme—redemption.
- The Bible has one hero—the Lord Jesus.
- The Bible has one villain—the devil.
- The Bible has one purpose—the glory of God!

All of its parts fit together. Can you imagine taking forty different people over a period of sixteen hundred years from different countries and different occupations and telling them each to write independent of one another without having read what the others had written? Put that altogether and see what kind of a hodgepodge you would have! Yet you have this wonderful unity in the Word of God.

I have been seriously studying the Bible now for many years. Throughout this study I have not found hidden faults; I have found hidden treasures and affirmations. I find an amazing interconnectedness within the Word of God. It is astounding!

Not One Stone Too Many, Not One Too Few

Dr. R. A. Torrey gave this illustration—let me paraphrase it. Suppose in your city they decided to build a monument honoring all of the fifty states in the union. Stones are gathered from each state. For example, from my home state of Florida, they get coral stone; from Georgia perhaps they would get granite; from Indiana they get limestone; from Nevada, sandstone—all of the various kinds of stones in different colors.

Then let's suppose that these stones are cut into different shapes; some are square, some are rectangular, some are cylindrical, some have a pyramid shape, some are like a trapezoid, and some have shapes that don't even have a name. They are cut out in the quarry, put in crates, and shipped by barge, by rail, and by air to your city.

Workmen uncrate these stones and begin to put them together, and they all interface, and they all interlock. There is not one stone too many, not one stone too few. No stone needs to be built up; no stone needs to be shaved down. And when they're finished, it is a magnificent temple.

You are a thinking person. Would you say that happened by chance? No, any thinking person would say that it did not happen by chance. There would have to have been a master architect who, in his mind, could see that building and had sent out the specifications to the quarry. Is that not true?

You see, when we get this Book written over a period of sixteen hundred years, forty different authors, three different languages, by men from all different walks of life and bring it together, it makes one beautiful temple of God's truth. Nothing needs to be added or taken away or embellished. There it stands—one Book! We can't say that just happened, that it was just an accident. No! The unity of the Bible is one of the wonderful proofs of the inspiration of God's Word—that all Scripture is given by inspiration of God.

The Bible Must Be the Word of God Because of Its Fulfilled Prophecy

Let me give you another reason you can believe that the Bible is the Word of God, and this is one of the great, great proofs of the inspiration of the Bible. It is the fulfilled prophecy of the Bible. This book, the Bible, has predictions of things that have yet to happen and will happen, because the Bible has predicted things that were predicted ahead of time and did happen. It has been wisely said that you can take a child of God, put him in a dungeon with a Bible and a candle and lock him away, and he will know more about what's going on in today's world with the Word of God than all the pundits in Washington. It's amazing to see history fit into the sockets of prophecy and, as you will see, actually fulfill prophecy.

We could study all kinds of fulfilled prophecy, but let's just take those related to the person and nature of Christ. Think about the Scriptures and the prophecies that were fulfilled just in the Lord Jesus Christ alone. Scholars say that Jesus fulfilled more than three hundred Old Testament prophecies. His enemies will say, "Oh sure, He fulfilled all these prophecies, but He rigged it! He just arranged that He would fulfill these prophecies." Well, if you believe that, let me tell you some of the things that He arranged.

First, He arranged to be born in Bethlehem. Could you arrange where you were going to be born? Micah 5:2 tells the prophecy that was fulfilled in Matthew 2:1–5. Then He managed for Isaiah to record details about His life seven hundred years before He was born. You can read the way Isaiah described Him in Isaiah 7, Isaiah 9, and Isaiah 53. Did you arrange to have the history of your life written before you were born?

Then He arranged to be crucified by execution on a cross. Did you know that if you read Psalm 22, written by David centuries before Jesus was born, you will read a description of the crucifixion of Jesus Christ that is written like a man who is standing at the foot of the cross? It tells about the piercing of His hands and feet, the gambling for His garments, the very words that Jesus would say upon the cross. Jesus wasn't looking back and quoting David; rather David was looking forward and quoting Jesus. It is an amazing thing that it is written as if somebody is an eyewitness to Christ's crucifixion.

This one psalm contains thirty-three direct prophecies that were fulfilled at Calvary, yet written a thousand years before the birth of Christ. And even more intriguing, when David wrote this prophecy, the form of capital punishment practiced by the Jews was stoning, not crucifixion. The Romans had not even come into power. Crucifixion was a Roman form of execution, and yet you find crucifixion described in Psalm 22.

Did He arrange that He would be crucified between two thieves? The Bible prophesied all of this in Isaiah 53:9–12; it was fulfilled as recorded in Matthew 27. The Bible prophesied that Judas would betray Him for exactly thirty pieces of silver in Zechariah 11:12. You can read about the fulfillment in Matthew 26:15.

And here is the classic "arrangement": He arranged to arise from the dead and be seen by more than five hundred witnesses. Some claim the apostles were hallucinating. Five hundred hallucinating at the same time? Having the same hallucination? Are people willing to die for a lie? No. People might live for a lie, but nobody will willingly die for a lie if they know that it is a lie. The early followers laid down their lives for the faith.

Most of these prophecies were not fulfilled by His friends but by His enemies, those who had the most to lose by the fulfillment of these prophecies. Matthew 26:56: "But all this was done that the Scriptures of the prophets might be fulfilled." Fulfilled prophecy is an incredible proof of the inspiration of the Bible.

The Bible Is Shown to Be the Word of God Because of Its Ever-Living Quality

The Bible is not the Book of the Month; it is the Book of the Ages. There is no book that has had as much opposition as the Bible. Men have laughed at it, they have scorned it, they have ridiculed it, they have made laws against it. There was a time in Scottish history when to own a Bible was a crime worthy of death. There are those who have vowed and declared that they will destroy this Book.

Peter declares, "All flesh is as grass, and all the glory of man as the flower of grass." You and I are just like a blade of grass sitting here; we are going to wither and die. "But the word of the Lord endures forever" (1 Pet. 1:24–25). Forever! We have some theological experts who think they have been called upon to reexamine the Bible. As far as I'm concerned, we ought to reexamine them. The Word of the Lord endures forever. The Bible is to judge us; we're not to judge the Bible. If you throw the old Book in the fiery furnace, it will come out without even the smell of smoke in its clothes.

Here we are in a new and a modern age, and we are still studying this old, old Book. It has stood the test of time and towers over all other books. God has kept the promise made to Isaiah more than twenty-five hundred years ago: "'As for Me,' says the LORD, 'this is My covenant with them: My Spirit who is upon you, and My words which I have put in your mouth, shall not depart from your mouth, nor from the mouth of your descendants, nor from the mouth of your descendants' descendants,' says the LORD, 'from this time and forevermore'" (Isa. 59:21).

The Bible Is Shown to Be the Word of God Because of Its Transforming Power

Finally, let's consider the transforming power of the Word of God. It is a compelling reason you can be certain the Bible is the Word of God. The great apostle Paul said in Romans 1:16, "For I am not ashamed of the gospel of Christ, for it is the power of God unto salvation." Hebrews 4:12 (KJV) says, "For the word of God is *quick* and powerful." That word *quick* is the word we get *zoo* and *zoology* from. It means it is alive; it pulsates with life and power. "The word of God is quick and *powerful*." The word *powerful* is the word *energes,* the word we get *energy* from. There's life and there's energy in the Bible. We read other books while this Book reads us. It is incredible. It is saving to the sinner. I have used this Book so many times to lead people to Christ and have seen them transformed.

Billy Graham started his ministry as a young man, and often when he preached, he would say, "The Bible says, . . . the Bible says." In 1954, he went to London to preach in the great Harringay Arena. A great crowd was there, including many news reporters. Two men who had come to see the flamboyant American evangelist were sitting up in the stands and discussing Billy Graham. One of the men was a medical doctor. They were finding fault with most everything.

Yet when Billy Graham began to preach, the Word of God began to take its toll. God says, "Is not My word . . . like a hammer that breaks the rock in pieces?" (Jer. 23:29). The hammer began to fall and conviction fell on that place, and that medical doctor who had been ridiculing Billy Graham said to the man sitting next to him: "I don't know about you, but I'm going down there to give my heart to Christ." And the man next to him said, "Yes, and I'll go with you, and here's your billfold, I'm a pickpocket."

Later Graham stated, "I found in my preaching that the Word of God was like a rapier; and when I quoted it under the power of the Holy Spirit, I could slay everything before me."

That's the incredible power of the Word of God to "rescue the perishing" and "care for the dying" and "snatch them in pity from sin and the grave." I *know* personally the transforming power of the Word of God—it's changed my life.

- It is saving for the sinner. It will stir the conscience, convict the mind, and convert the soul.
- It is sweet for the saint. So many times I have found treasure and peace in the Word of God. Oh, how precious are the words of God.
- It is sufficient for the sufferer. How many times people have pillowed their head on the precious promises of the Word of God. I feel sorry for people who do not have a Bible to lean on.
- It is satisfying to the scholar. I have studied this Book, and I would never even dream of saying I've come to the bottom of the Word of God. Someone said the Word of God is so deep that the scholars can swim and never touch bottom and yet so precious that a little child can come and get a drink without fear of drowning. Thank God for the Bible, the Word of God.

You can trust the Bible. You will never be a great Christian until you come to the unshakable conviction that the Bible is the Word of God.

2

Every Christian Ought to Know

THE ASSURANCE OF SALVATION

Whoever believes that Jesus is the Christ is born of God, and everyone who loves Him who begot also loves him who is begotten of Him. By this we know that we love the children of God, when we love God and keep His commandments. For this is the love of God, that we keep His commandments. And His commandments are not burdensome. For whatever is born of God overcomes the world. And this is the victory that has overcome the world— our faith. Who is he who overcomes the world, but he who believes that Jesus is the Son of God?

This is He who came by water and blood—Jesus Christ; not only by water, but by water and blood. And it is the Spirit who bears witness, because the Spirit is truth. For there are three that bear witness in heaven: the Father, the Word, and the Holy Spirit; and these three are one. And there are three that bear witness on earth: the Spirit, the water, and the blood; and these three agree as one.

If we receive the witness of men, the witness of God is greater; for this is the witness of God which He has testified of His Son. He who believes in the Son of God has the witness in himself; he who does not believe God has made Him a liar, because he has not believed the testimony that God has given of His Son. And this is the testimony: that God has given us eternal life, and this life is in His Son. He who has the Son has life; he who does not have the Son of God does not have life. These things I have written to you who believe in the name of the Son of God, that you may know that you have eternal life.

1 JOHN 5:1–13

One basic thing every Christian ought to know beyond the shadow of any doubt is that he or she is saved. Now what does it mean to be saved? First, it means that every sin is forgiven and buried in the grave of God's forgetfulness. Second, it means that Jesus Christ through the Holy Spirit comes to live in us—to give us peace, power, and purpose. Third, it means that when we die or when Jesus comes again, we are going home to heaven to be with Him.

Every Christian needs the absolute assurance that he or she has had this experience of salvation. It is much better to be a shouting Christian than a doubting Christian. We ought not walk around like a question mark with our heads bent over but like an exclamation mark. We should not be saying, "I hope I am saved," or, "I think I am saved," but, "Praise God, I know that I know that I am saved."

You Can *Know without a Doubt*

I was making a ministry call in the hospital. A lady was dying, and I had been called to her bedside to pray for her. I asked her if she had the assurance of salvation. She answered, "No." I asked her if she wanted to be saved. She said, "Indeed I do." So I explained to her from the Word of God how to be saved, and then I led her in a prayer. She prayed and asked Jesus Christ to forgive her sins, to come into her heart and save her. Of course, I thought this was wonderful. Here was a precious lady who in just a little while is going into the presence of God, and now she has that blessed assurance of salvation.

I turned to some of her family members who were there and said, "Isn't it wonderful that she has been saved and is going to heaven?" Her son-in-law said, "Nobody can know that she is saved."

I took my Bible and turned to 1 John 5:13 and read, "These things I have written to you who believe in the name of the Son of God, that you may know that you have eternal life, and that you may continue to believe in the name of the Son of God." I asked the man, "Do you see the word *know* in that verse?" I said, "Of course, we can know that we have eternal life." Someone has well said, "If you could have salvation and not know it, you could lose it and not miss it." The truth of the matter is, if you have genuine salvation, you should know it; and if it is real, thank God you can never lose it.

When we are talking about the assurance of salvation, we are talking about something of vital importance. We are not talking about denominational preference, the height of the church steeple, or the color of the carpet. We are talking about the eternal destiny of the human soul. We are talking about your ever-living, never-dying soul. We ought to have absolute certainty about some things. To be victorious in your Christian life, you need to be able to say, "I know that I am saved. I know that I am heaven born and heaven bound."

Can You Be Saved and Have Doubts about It?

But is it possible to be saved and to have doubts about it? If it is not possible for the child of God to sometimes be beleaguered with doubts, then why did the Apostle John write, "These things I have written to you who believe in the name of the Son of God that you may know that you have eternal life." Evidently some were having serious questions and doubts about their salvation. Perhaps others thought they were saved but were not truly saved.

Doubt doesn't necessarily mean that you haven't been saved. As a matter of fact, we only tend to doubt that which we believe. Doubt is to your spirit what pain is to your body. Pain doesn't mean that one is dead. Pain means that there is life but that something is wrong. A part of the body is not functioning as it ought.

And so doubt is possible but not profitable. I have never known of any Christian who was really effective in his or her service to the Lord who did not have the full assurance of his or her salvation. Yet we must admit that Christians can have doubts and still be saved. However, it seems to me that they are going to heaven second-class.

I Doubt You've Been Saved

One lady told an evangelist, "I have been saved for twenty-five years and never had a doubt." He said, "I doubt you have been saved." That would be like a person saying, "We have been married for twenty-five years and never had an argument." Indeed we may have doubts. Doubts are not good in salvation, nor are arguments good in marriage. Pain is not good in our bodies, but these are the facts of life.

But I remind you that if you are trying to live the Christian life with doubts, it is much like driving an automobile with the brakes on. You need to have not a hope-so, think-so, maybe-so but a wonderful know-so salvation.

In this chapter I am going to stay primarily in the little epistle of 1 John, and in that small book, John uses the word *know* or *known* thirty-eight times. John is writing that we might *know* that we have eternal life—so we can call it the Book of Assurance.

Assurance Begins with the New Birth

"Whoever believes that Jesus is the Christ is born of God, and everyone who loves Him who begot also loves him who is begotten of Him" (1 John 5:1).

Being born spiritually is much like being born physically. One thing about birth is that it makes a perfect example of salvation because all of us have experienced a physical birth and can relate to the facts of a birth.

John's Gospel gives us clear teaching about this birth:

> There was a man of the Pharisees named
> Nicodemus, a ruler of the Jews. This man came to
> Jesus by night and said to Him, "Rabbi, we know that
> You are a teacher come from God; for no one can do
> these signs that You do unless God is with him."
>
> Jesus answered and said to him, "Most assuredly,
> I say to you, unless one is born again, he cannot see
> the kingdom of God."
>
> Nicodemus said to Him, "How can a man be born
> when he is old? Can he enter a second time into his
> mother's womb and be born?"
>
> Jesus answered, "Most assuredly, I say to you,
> unless one is born of water and the Spirit, he cannot
> enter the kingdom of God. That which is born of the
> flesh is flesh, and that which is born of the Spirit is
> spirit. Do not marvel that I said to you, 'You must be
> born again.'" (John 3:1–7)

In this passage Jesus was talking to a religious man named
Nicodemus. Nicodemus wanted to know about miracles. In essence
Jesus told him that in order for him to understand miracles, he himself needed to become a miracle. He needed to be born again. He
asked Jesus about this. In his answer to Nicodemus, Jesus points out
some things about the new birth that we need to understand for full
assurance.

In a birth, a conception takes place. In verse 5, Jesus said that
we are born of water and the Spirit in order to enter into the

kingdom of God. Water speaks of the Word of God,[1] and the Spirit means the Spirit of God. When the Spirit of God and the Word of God come together in the womb of faith, there is wonderful conception. It will not happen without our consent. We must provide the womb of faith.

In a birth, a continuation is involved. Verse 6 tells us that physical life is imparted by physical life, and spiritual life is imparted by spiritual life.

Parents do not manufacture babies in the true sense of the word. They pass on the life that has been given to them. Life is transmitted.

Likewise in the new birth, the life of God is transmitted into us. The term "born again" literally means "born from above." Salvation is not only getting man out of earth into heaven but *getting God out of heaven* into man through His Spirit.

In a birth, a character is produced. In the flesh we receive the nature of our fleshly parents. When the Spirit of God and the Word of God create in us something supernatural, we receive the character of a new being with a divine nature.

Christians are not just nice people; they are new creatures. We are not like a tadpole that becomes a frog. We are more like a frog who has become a prince by the kiss of grace.

In a birth, a completion transpires. A birth is a once-for-all experience in the natural realm and also in the spiritual realm.

When a baby is born in earthly society, a record is written down. In heaven a new name is written down in glory. This speaks of a completed fact.

It is important that we understand this because no one can ever be unborn. Even when one's body ceases to exist, the spirit of an individual goes on timeless, dateless, and measureless throughout all eternity.

In a birth a commencement occurs. A birth is a starting place. A little child is all tomorrows. He has no past. No policemen will be there ready to arrest a newborn baby for crimes he has done. When we come to Jesus, we are not yesterdays—we are all tomorrows.

Having said that, however, we then commence to grow. When the baby is born, it has all of the equipment that it will ever have. Now it needs to grow. What a blessing to discover, develop, and deploy what we've received in our new birth!

In a birth a certainty is expected. A birth is a definite experience. If I were to ask you this question, "Have you ever been born?" it would almost seem nonsensical to ask it. But suppose I did ask it, and you were to answer, "I hope so. I'm doing the best I can." Or even more ridiculous, you would say, "I have always been born."

No, there is indeed a certainty implied by a birth. There was a time when you were not born, and there was a time when you were.

Let's talk about our part in the new birth. We had no choice about our first birth, but we have one about our second birth. As I said previously, we provide the womb of faith. "Whoever believes that Jesus is the Christ is born of God" (1 John 5:1). The new birth takes place when we believe on the Lord Jesus Christ.

The crystal clear and classic passage that relates to this is Ephesians 2:8–9, which says, "For by grace you have been saved through faith, and that not of yourselves; it is the gift of God, not of works, lest anyone should boast."

This passage is so great because here the Scripture clearly delineates what saves us, and then in contradistinction so we can make no mistake at all about it, it speaks of what does not save us. Therefore, we can look at it, first of all, negatively and see what doesn't save and then positively and see what does.

These verses tell us that self and works do not save. "Not of yourself." "Not of works." That seems simple enough, doesn't it? But most people do not understand that simple concept. If you asked the average man on the street, "Are you going to heaven?" "Sure!" "Why?" "I'm doing the best I can." Think about that answer. I (self) am doing (works) the best I can.

God Is Not Santa Claus

Many think that God is like Santa Claus—making a list, checking it twice, finding out who's naughty or nice. Then they think one day at the judgment we will stand before Him and He is going to weigh the good we've done against the bad and see which side the balance comes down on. Most people believe they can behave themselves into heaven.

But look at our Scripture again clearly. "Not of yourselves . . . not of works" (Eph. 2:8–9). It is not of self, and it is not of works. The devil doesn't give up easily and will encourage you to believe something like this: "Yes, I cannot work my way to heaven, but works will help. It is the grace of God *plus* what I do. I do my part and God does His."

We're Not Going to Heaven in a Rowboat

I've heard this illustration used by those who believe in works plus grace: If you were rowing across a stream in a rowboat and pulled on one oar—we will call that "works"—you go around in a circle. But if you pull on the other oar—we will call that "faith"— you go around in a circle in the opposite direction. But then with a wise look on their face, they say both oars—faith *and* works—will get you across the stream. That may sound like a good illustration, but it has a fatal flaw: *we are not going to heaven in a rowboat!* We are going to heaven by the grace of God. It is not of self, and it is not of works.

If you don't understand that, you will never have the assurance of your salvation. If one small part depends on you, you will never have assurance. If any of it depends on your works, you will never know if you have done enough. Get this into your heart and head; it is not of self and not of works.

Now look at Ephesians 2:8 again carefully. "For by grace you have been saved through faith." On the positive side, it is grace through faith.

Now what is grace? Grace is the characteristic of God's nature that makes God love sinners such as we. God does not love us because we are valuable; we are valuable because He loves us. That love is by His sheer grace. Grace is something we do not deserve at all. It is God's unmerited love and favor shown to sinners who deserve judgment.

Grace—God's Riches at Christ's Expense

Here is a way to help understand what *grace* means. Let's make an acrostic out of it: G-R-A-C-E, "**G**od's **R**iches **A**t **C**hrist's **E**xpense." That's grace. When you think of grace, think of Jesus dying in agony and blood upon the cross for undeserving sinners. We have nothing to commend us to God. We are sinners by birth, choice, and practice, but God loves us in spite of our sin, and that love is called grace.

Grace is one of the most beautiful words in our language. When people understand grace, they want to write songs about it like "Amazing Grace."

Faith—Forsaking All I Trust Him

If grace is God's riches at Christ's expense, what is faith? Here is another acrostic: F-A-I-T-H, "Forsaking All I Trust Him." I forsake dependence on my good intentions, my good deeds, my own so-called sense of self-worth, and I also forsake my sin. I turn my back on sin and I trust Him. I put my faith where God has put my sins—on the Lord Jesus Christ.

This faith is not a mere intellectual belief; the demons believe and tremble (James 2:19). No, it is more than belief. It is commitment. I can believe an airplane can fly, but I don't truly trust it until I get in it.

Here is how salvation works and the new birth comes about. I put my faith in God's grace. It is not the faith that saves; it is the grace that saves. Faith just lays hold of that grace. Think of grace as God's hand of love reaching down from heaven, saying, "I love you. I want to save you." It is a nail-pierced hand because He has paid for our sins. Think of faith as your sin-stained hand, saying, "God, I need you. I want you." And when you put your hand of faith in God's hand of grace, that is salvation. "For by grace you have been saved through faith, and that not of yourselves; it is the gift of God."

Grace Is a Gift

If you pay anything for a gift, then it ceases to be a gift. Suppose you have a friend named Jim who tells you, "I am going to buy you a $50,000 automobile as a gift." He drives up in front of your house with that brand-new automobile. Suppose you were to say to him, "Jim, I can't let you do that. It is just too great a gift. Here is a quarter. Here is twenty-five cents; let me help pay for this thing." And so he pays $49,999.75, and you pay two bits. Now you are driving the car down the road, and someone says, "That is a nice car you have there." You say, "Yes, my friend Jim and I bought this car." That would be an insult to Jim, would it not?

A Disgrace to Grace

We must remember that we cannot take any praise or credit for our salvation. None whatsoever! It is all of God. It is a gift, and we cannot boast about it. There will be no peacocks strutting around in heaven. When we get to heaven, God gets all of the praise and all of the glory because of His marvelous, matchless, wonderful grace.

The Birthmarks of the Believer

We said that when we enter the kingdom it is through a new birth, and that comes about when we put our faith in the grace of God. John, in the epistle of 1 John, gives some traits of the twice born. We might call these the birthmarks of the believer. If we are born again, the evidence will be there. I want to take three of these evidences that John mentions in this small epistle. You may test your salvation by them.

Number 1. The Commandment Test

"Now by this we know that we know Him, if we keep His commandments. He who says, 'I know Him,' and does not keep His commandments, is a liar, and the truth is not in him. But whoever keeps His word, truly the love of God is perfected in him. By this we know that we are in Him. He who says he abides in Him ought himself also to walk just as He walked" (1 John 2:3–6).

John does not beat around the bush here. He says in effect, "Look, don't tell me you are saved if you are not keeping God's commandments. If you say you are, you are a liar."

Let me be clear. You are not saved because you keep the commandments, but you will keep the commandments if you are saved. We have learned already that salvation is not of works. You are not saved by "commandment keeping."

Now that brings up a serious problem because there is not a one of us who would dare say that since we have been saved we have always obeyed every commandment to perfection.

Keeping the Stars

The understanding of all this is that word *keep*. It comes from the Greek word *tereō*, and among its meanings is "to watch over." It was used in ancient times by sailors. Those early sailors did not have global positioning satellites and radio signals to guide them, yet they sailed over the trackless seas. In doing that they sailed by the stars. They kept their eye on the heavens, and they called that "keeping the stars."

Keeping the stars is much like keeping the commandments. Any sailor could occasionally get blown off course, get distracted and waver this way or that. Yet he is keeping the stars.

When we keep the commandments, we steer by them. That does not speak of sinless perfection because none is perfect except Jesus Christ. But it does mean that our heart's desire is to keep the Word of God. From the moment I gave my heart to Jesus Christ, there has been in me a desire to keep God's Word.

There are a couple more problem verses in 1 John. We might as well look at them full on. "Whoever abides in Him does not sin. Whoever sins has neither seen Him nor known Him" (1 John 3:6).

"He who sins is of the devil, for the devil has sinned from the beginning. For this purpose the Son of God was manifested, that He might destroy the works of the devil. Whoever has been born of God does not sin, for His seed remains in him; and he cannot sin, because he has been born of God" (1 John 3:8–9).

You might say, "I must not be saved because I know that the ability to sin is within me." Again we have to do a little study because there is an adequate answer. "He who sins" is in the present tense, and it speaks of a habitual course of action. John is saying that a man who is born of God does not make sin his practice, his lifestyle, his habit. It does not mean that he could not slip into sin.

May I give this testimony? Before I was saved, I was running to sin. Since being saved, I am running from it. I may fall, I may slip, I may fail, but my heart's desire is to live for God.

John is saying, "If you call yourself a Christian and you are not steering by God's commandments, and if you are living a habitually sinful life with no conviction, no compunction, no contrition, no disquietude, then don't call yourself a Christian because you are not."

Number 2. The Companion Test

"We know that we have passed from death to life, because we love the brethren. He who does not love his brother abides in death. Whoever hates his brother is a murderer, and you know that no murderer has eternal life abiding in him" (1 John 3:14–15). Remember that when we believe on the Lord Jesus Christ, we are born of God. Remember that we have a new nature, and it is God's nature. Also remember that we are in the family of God, and so we have brothers and sisters.

So if I am born of God and have become a partaker of His divine nature, love will automatically be in my heart, for God is love. To be God's child is to share God's nature. We don't need a bumper sticker or a lapel pin to prove that we are Christians. Jesus said, "By this will all men know that you are My disciples if you have love for one another" (John 13:35 NASB).

Love is the nature of God, and therefore it is characteristic of His children. If we love Him and His love is in us, then we are going to love what He loves, which is His dear family. This is the reason it is foolish to say yes to Jesus but no to His church. Many descriptions and analogies describe the church:

- The church is a **building**, and Christ is the foundation. Who could say yes to the foundation and no to the building that rests upon it?
- The church is His **bride**. Who could say yes to the groom and no to the bride?
- The church is His **body**. Who could say yes to Christ the head and then no to the body?

So one of the marks, the traits of the twice born, is that we love one another—the members of His church.

That doesn't mean that we are all lovable by nature. We are not by nature lovely. We are sinners. A church is comprised of people who have finally realized that they are sinners and banded themselves together to do something about it. It is the only organization I know of besides Hell's Angels that you have to profess to be bad before you can join. One must say, "I am a sinner, and I am turning my life over to Jesus Christ."

Therefore, all of us are in various stages in our spiritual growth and sanctification. Those in the church with us who are steering by the stars may be temporarily off course, they may fail, but they are onboard with us, and they are our brothers and sisters. To love Jesus is to love His church. To persecute His church is to persecute Jesus.

A man named Saul, who later became the apostle Paul, was on the road to Damascus to arrest Christians. The Lord Jesus appeared to him in a blinding light and said, "Saul, Saul, why are you persecuting Me?" Saul could have said, "Whoever you are, I am not persecuting you; I am persecuting the church." The truth of the matter is, however, that when one persecutes the church, he is persecuting Jesus. To neglect the church is to neglect Jesus; to love the church is to love Jesus. That kind of love is a birthmark of the believer.

Number 3. The Confidence Test

"He who believes in the Son of God has the witness in himself; he who does not believe God has made Him a liar, because he has not believed the testimony that God has given of His Son" (1 John 5:10). This is the greatest and strongest test. All of the others grow out of it.

Biblical belief (confidence) is not just an intellectual exercise. You do not believe *about* Jesus; you believe *in* Jesus. You can believe an airplane can fly, but you trust it when you get onboard. Again I remind you that it is more than an intellectual assent to some facts that saves us.

Notice also that this verse is in the present tense. It doesn't say, "He who has believed"; it says, "He who *believes.*" Our confidence is always to be in the present tense.

Sometimes the question is asked, "Are you saved?" The answer comes, "Yes I am saved. I remember walking down the aisle when I was nine years old, giving my hand to my pastor and my heart to Jesus Christ. I may not be living for God right now. I'll admit that. But I know I'm saved because I remember what I did when I was a nine-year-old boy. I remember believing on Jesus Christ."

The Bible never uses such an experience as proof of salvation. It never points us back to some time when we may have believed on Jesus Christ. It always deals with our present confidence.

It is interesting how many people want to go back to an event in the past. Some even say, "If you cannot show me the place and tell me the moment when you received Jesus Christ as your personal Savior and Lord, then you are not saved." There is just one thing wrong with that; it is not biblical and not so.

The Bible never says that you will know you are saved by something you remember in the past. It says, "He that believes." Present tense! It is simple. If you are believing, you did believe.

The question is, Are you believing in Jesus right now? Some true believers are concerned because they cannot remember the exact time like others can. Some had a cataclysmic experience when they turned in faith from sin to Christ. Others grew up in a Christian family and were nurtured along until one day it dawned on them that they were trusting Jesus as their personal Lord and Savior. That doesn't mean they were half saved and then three-quarters saved and then all the way saved. No one is half saved. To be half saved is to be altogether lost. There was a time when they came to saving faith, but they may not be able to pinpoint that particular time like others can do.

How Do We Know We Are in Georgia?

Let me illustrate. Suppose we are both in Orlando, Florida, and we are going to Atlanta, Georgia. You drive to Atlanta and I fly. I ask you to meet me in Atlanta and to pick me up at the airport. When you drive, you will know when you cross the state line. It will be obvious because a sign will be there that says, "Welcome to Georgia." When I fly, I will cross the same line, but I will not be aware of it. But I will land in the Atlanta airport. We meet in the Atlanta airport, and we are both there. I came in an airplane, and you came in an automobile. You give your testimony and say, "I remember exactly when I crossed the state line." My testimony is, "I don't remember when I crossed the state line, but I know I did because I am in the Atlanta airport. The important thing is that *since* I am in the Atlanta airport, I know I *must* be in Georgia and *did* cross that line."

If you *are* trusting Jesus, you *did* trust Jesus. The real test is not whether you remember the time or the place but that you are this moment putting your confidence in the Lord Jesus Christ.

The story is told of Will Rogers who one time went in to get a passport, and the official said, "We need your birth certificate." And he said, "What for?" They said, "For proof of your birth." He said, "Well I'm here, ain't I?" That makes the point for me. If you *are* trusting Jesus—present tense—you are saved. If not, don't rely on some past experience.

This brings another question. How can we know if we are truly believing at this moment?

The Witness of the Spirit

First, there is the witness of the Spirit. "He who believes in the Son of God has the witness in himself" (1 John 5:10). The witness of the Spirit is not an emotional feeling. Your emotions are the shallowest part of your nature. Salvation is the deepest work of God. He will not do the deepest work in the shallowest part. The witness of the Spirit is the Holy Spirit speaking to your human spirit with a quiet confidence that you belong to Jesus Christ. It is an inner awareness that those who are saved know that they are. A true believer with this witness is never at the mercy of an unbeliever who has an argument.

The Witness of the Word

The second witness is the witness of the Word. "And this is the testimony: that God has given us eternal life, and this life is in His Son. He who has the Son has life; he who does not have the Son of God does not have life. These things I have *written to you who believe* in the name of the Son of God, that you may *know* that you have eternal life" (1 John 5:11–13). The Scripture is given to us that we may know.

One night while out sharing Jesus Christ, I asked a man if he wanted to receive Christ as his personal Lord and Savior. He did, and after we prayed together, I said, "I want to give you your spiritual birth certificate." I turned to John 5:24 and read, "Most assuredly, I say to you, he who hears My word and believes in Him who sent Me has everlasting life, and shall not come into judgment, but has passed from death into life."

I read it slowly and said, "This is Jesus who is speaking. Do you believe this?"

"Yes," he said.

"'He who hears My word.' Have you heard His word?"

"Yes."

"'And believes in Him who sent Me.' Have you believed on the God that sent the Lord Jesus?"

"Yes."

"'Has everlasting life.' Do you have everlasting life?"

"I hope so," he said.

I said, "Let's read it again." And we did. Again he answered yes to every question but the last. Again he said, "I hope so." "Let's read it again," I said. This time when I asked him if he had everlasting life, the light went on inside. "Why, yes! Yes!" he shouted. "Who says so?" "God says so! God says so!" That is the confidence of the Word. Put them together; the witness of the Spirit and the witness of the Scripture give us this glad certainty.

Let me say before you read any further that if you have never received Jesus Christ as your personal Lord and Savior, you may do so right now. By an act of faith, trust Him to save you. He is ready and willing and will do it this very moment. Don't look for a sign and don't ask for a feeling; stand on His Word.

If you are saved and have doubts, don't look back to some past experience. Ask yourself this moment: Am I trusting Jesus? If not, trust Him right now. If you are trusting, there will be the genuine birthmarks in your life. There will be a desire to obey His commandments, there will be a love for His people, and there will be a quiet confidence witnessed by the Holy Spirit and the Bible that you belong to Him.

My Personal Testimony

As a young teen I gave my heart to Christ, but I did not have it explained to me as I have explained it to you. For some months I was up and down. I didn't know whether I was lost and the Holy Spirit had me under conviction or I was saved and the devil was trying to make me doubt it.

I had walked my girlfriend home and stopped at the corner of Calvin Avenue and 39th Street in West Palm Beach, Florida. I wanted to get it settled. I looked up into the starry sky, wanting to look into the face of God. I said, "O God, I don't have assurance. I am going to get it settled tonight, once and for all, now and forever."

I prayed this way, "Lord Jesus, with all my heart, I trust You to save me. I don't look for a sign, and I don't ask for a feeling. I stand on Your Word and You cannot lie. I trust You to save me." I continued to pray, "Lord, if I was saved before, this can't take it away, but if I wasn't, I am driving down a peg tonight. This settles it forever." A river of peace started to flow in my heart, and it is still flowing right now.

Blessed Assurance

If you do that and still have doubts, do you know what is probably wrong? You have got some sin in your life. You are not obeying the Lord, and you need to confess that sin because there is nothing more damaging to faith and confidence than unconfessed, unrepented sin in your heart and in your life. Deal with that sin and see if the confidence of your salvation does not return!

Thank God for a know-so salvation.

3

Every Christian Ought to Know

ABOUT ETERNAL SECURITY

*My sheep hear My voice, and I know them, and
they follow Me. And I give them eternal life, and
they shall never perish; neither shall anyone
snatch them out of My hand. My Father, who has
given them to Me, is greater than all; and no one
is able to snatch them out of My Father's hand.*

JOHN 10:27–29

Is there anything better than being saved? Now, be careful how
you answer because it's a loaded question. Yes, there's something

better than being saved: It is being saved and knowing that you're saved, having that blessed assurance. Well, is there anything better than being saved and knowing you're saved? Yes, there is! It is being saved, knowing that you're saved, and knowing that you can never *ever* lose your salvation.

If that proposition is true, you will have to admit that is indeed wonderful: That you could be saved—heaven born and heaven bound, that you can have the absolute assurance that you're saved, and that you can know that you can never ever lose your salvation. Well, I want to show you that, indeed, it is true!

Sometimes eternal security is looked upon as a denominational doctrine. Let's go past that. It doesn't make any difference what any denomination believes if it is not Bible based. We're going to see what the Bible has to say about eternal security. If the Bible says it, we're going to believe it. If the Bible doesn't say it, then we have no authority to believe it. The doctrine of eternal security is not incidental; it is absolutely fundamental to your Christian life for several reasons.

Spiritual Health

First, you need to have this assurance for your spiritual health. Can you imagine a little child in a family who does not know from one day to the next whether he may be in the family? Perhaps one day he was naughty and disobeyed, and so he's no longer a member of the family. Then after several weeks he repents and gets right again, and he is received back into the family. He has his bedroom again, and he can see his mother and daddy again and brother and sister again. Then after a while he's out of the family again—that's not my daddy, that's not my mother, that's not my brother, that's not my sister, that's not my house. Can you imagine what an emotional wreck the child would be if he went through that?

I know Christians who are emotional wrecks because they do not have the assurance that they are children of God. They're in the family and then out of the family, then in the family and out of the family.

Your Productivity

I know few Christians who are spiritually productive who do not have the assurance of their salvation and understand that they are eternally secure. Why is this? Very simple—when we know that the future is secure, then we can concentrate on the present.

In 1937, the Golden Gate Bridge was built in San Francisco, spanning that great bay. I have seen that bridge; it's a marvel and a wonder. It was a dangerous, treacherous thing to work on that bridge, as it began to rise hundreds of feet above the icy swirling waters of San Francisco Bay. The workmen were afraid for their lives. Some of them fell and drowned; in all, twenty-three people there lost their lives in accidental deaths.

Management said, "We've got to do something about that," so they built a safety net underneath the workers. They spent $100,000 building this net, and when they built the safety net, they found out it really wasn't an expense. It was a great saving, because the work went 25 percent faster, and far fewer lives were lost. As a matter of fact, only ten, fewer than half as many, fell in the net, and of course their lives were saved.

Why could these people work with more productivity? Because of their security! They knew that the net was there. And that's the way it is in the Christian life.

I'm not endeavoring to keep myself safe; I know I am saved. I'm saved by the grace of God; therefore I can be productive with grateful service. *When we are confident of the future, we can concentrate on the present.*

Aid in Evangelism

A lot of people would like to be saved, but they think, *Well, I just can't live it. I can't hold out. I know how weak I am.* They're just afraid that they would go forward in the church, profess to be a Christian, and then fall away and look foolish.

How wonderful to tell these people that the God who saves them is the God who will keep them. It's a great tool in evangelism—sharing the Lord Jesus Christ.

They Never Were a Christian in the First Place

What do we mean by *eternal security*? We don't mean that once a person joins a church and gets baptized she's eternally secure because she may or may not be saved. We're talking about somebody who has become a partaker of the divine nature, somebody who is heaven born and therefore heaven bound, a person who has had a new birth, a person who has become genuinely a child of God.

Sometimes when I teach on this subject of the new birth, somebody will say, "I know somebody who used to be a Christian who is no longer a Christian." I just say, "Well, you think you know somebody who used to be a Christian and is no longer a Christian. Maybe he never was a Christian, or maybe he still is a Christian. You are not equipped to judge."

I Never Knew You

Many people look like Christians and act like Christians, but they've never been saved. An interesting verse is Matthew 7:22. Jesus is talking about the final judgment: "Many will say to Me in that day, 'Lord, Lord [Now that's the proper profession; they call him Lord!], have we not prophesied in Your name [The word *prophesy* means to speak for God; evidently these were preachers!], cast out demons in Your name [claiming that they were exorcising demons from people], and done many wonders in Your name?'" [Maybe they sang in the choir, took up the offering, or taught Sunday school.] And then Jesus says in the next verse, "And then will I declare to them, 'I never knew you; depart from Me, you who practice lawlessness!'" He didn't say, "Oh, you had it, but you lost it." He says instead, "I *never* knew you."

You say that person used to be a Christian and no longer is because you heard him prophesy, you saw him do all these wonderful works. But he didn't lose his salvation. He never had it!

Let me give you a verse in contradistinction to Matthew 7:22–23. It's John 10:27–28. Jesus said, "My sheep hear My voice, and I know them, and they follow Me." In the Matthew passage He said, "I never knew you." This time He says, "My sheep hear My voice, and I know them, and they follow Me. And I give them eternal life, and they shall never perish." You see the difference: Some are religious, but they never were saved; the others were saved, and they will never perish. Those who fall away never were truly saved.

Another key verse is 1 John 2:19. It talks about those who begin for a while and then they go away from the faith. This verse explains it: "They went out from us, but they were not of us; for if they had been of us, they would [no doubt] have continued with us; but they went out that they might be made manifest, that none of them were of us." These people start out for God, continue awhile, and then they go back to the old way. Somebody says, "They lost their salvation." John says, "No, they went out from us because they were not of us. Had they been of us, they would no doubt have continued with us." Here's a saying I like that sums it up:

The faith that fizzles before the finish had a flaw from the first.

They never really knew the Lord.

I want to give you some reasons I believe in the eternal security of the believer.

God's Sacred Promise

God has made a sacred promise to you. It is found in Romans 8:38–39. This is going to be one of the most all-inclusive statements you will ever read—in the Bible or out of the Bible. Pay close attention. Paul is going to tell us ten strong opponents that can never separate us from God's love. "For I am persuaded that neither death nor life, nor angels nor principalities nor powers, nor things present nor things to come, nor height nor depth, nor any other created thing, shall be able to separate us from the love of God which is in Christ Jesus our Lord."

Notice these opponents:
- Death
- Life
- Angels
- Principalities
- Powers
- Things present

- Things to come
- Height
- Depth
- Any other creature

That's powerful, isn't it? He is saying there is *nothing* that can separate us from the love of God. That is a sacred promise. It is a wonderfully inclusive verse.

I challenge you, the reader, to name any force that may separate us from God's love that Paul failed to mention.

God's Determined Purpose

In Philippians 1:6, the apostle Paul says this: "Being confident of this very thing, that He who has begun a good work in you will complete it." Paul was confident of this—that which God starts, He will finish. God is the One who saves us. Salvation is the work of God; it is not "do it yourself." Who began a good work in us? The Holy Spirit of God! He was the *Convictor.* Do you think that you were convicted of your sin by yourself? No, the Bible says, "There is none who seeks after God" (Rom. 3:11). He's the One who ran you down and convicted you of your sin. If He couldn't run faster than you could run, you never would have been saved. "We love Him because He first loved us" (1 John 4:19).

Not only is He the Convictor, but also He is the *Convertor.* He was the one who opened our understanding. That's the reason I pray before I preach. Anything I can talk you into, somebody else can talk you out of. Anything that the Holy Spirit gives you is yours.

He is the Convictor and the Convertor, and therefore, He is the *Completor.* Have you ever started anything you couldn't finish?

When I was a little boy, I used to build model airplanes. I don't think I ever finished one of them. That's just a character flaw on my part. Many of us start things we just can't finish.

I heard one time that Billy and Jimmy were talking, and Billy said to Jimmy, "My daddy has a list of men that he can whip, and your dad's name is number one on the list." Jimmy went home and told his daddy, "Daddy, did you know that Billy's dad has a list of men that he can whip, and your name is number one on the list?" Jimmy's daddy said, "Is that so?" Jimmy said, "That's what I heard." Jimmy's daddy went over to Billy's daddy and knocked on the door. Jimmy's daddy said, "My son Jimmy said that your son Billy said that you have a list of men you can whip, and my name is number one on that list. Is that right?" Billy's daddy said, "Yes, that's right." Jimmy's daddy said, "Well, I don't believe you can do it. What are you going to do about that?" Billy's daddy said, "Well, I'll just take your name off the list."

God never has to take our name off the list. God never starts something that He can't finish. I thank God for that. Look at this verse again: "Being confident of this very thing, that He who has begun a good work in you will complete it." If salvation is *your* work, maybe it will run out in a ditch somewhere; but if it's *God's* work, it will be completed. It's wonderful. Let me give you another reason.

God's Sovereign Predestination

You are already predestined to be like Jesus. We're in deep theology here, but let's see what the Bible says in Romans 8:29–30: "For whom He foreknew [He knew you were going to be saved before you were ever saved], He also predestined to be conformed to the image of His Son, that He might be the firstborn among many brethren. Moreover whom He predestined, these He also called; whom He called, these He also justified; and whom He justified, these He also glorified."

God has a plan for you: you're going to be like Jesus. God looked before you were ever born. He saw you receiving Christ as your personal Savior and Lord. He said, "That one's going to be like Jesus." "For whom He foreknew, He also predestined." Do you know what "predestined" means? It means your destiny is already determined. You are predestined to be like Jesus. If you're predestined to be like Jesus, will you be like Jesus? (It's all right to say yes. It would be wrong to say no.) If you're predestined to be like Jesus, *of course* you will be like Jesus. What is foreknown in heaven cannot be annulled by hell. It's predestined; *it is settled!*

Read the verse again: "For whom He foreknew [He knew you were going to be saved before you were ever saved.], He also predestined to be conformed to the image of His Son, that He might be the firstborn among many brethren. Moreover whom He predestined, these He also called; whom He called, these He also justified; and whom He justified, these He also glorified." We would expect him to say, "He will glorify." However, God already sees you glorified before it happens because we live *in* history, but He lives *above and beyond* history. God sees you already glorified in heaven. Well, if that is true, and it is true of course, obviously you're predestined to be like the Lord Jesus Christ.

You might say, "I don't feel so glorified right now." He's not finished with you. But He has begun a good work, and what He has begun, He will complete. You are predestined—if you are a believer—to be like the Lord Jesus Christ.

Calvary's Perfect Provision

The Bible says something wonderful in Hebrews 10:14: "For by one offering He [the Lord] has perfected forever those who are being sanctified." Notice the phrase "perfected forever." Jesus Christ hung upon that cross in agony never to die again. His one offering perfected forever those of us who are saved. Because of the perfect Sacrifice, we have complete perfection in the Lord Jesus Christ. When you get saved, God doesn't just give you a fresh start; He gives you eternal perfection by that "one offering."

Nowhere in the Bible can you find where anybody is ever saved twice. You can't find it. You couldn't find where anybody was saved twice any more than you could find where anybody was born physically two times. You're born physically once, and you're born spiritually once. You never find that being repeated. Why? Because "by one offering He has perfected [us] forever." When you were saved, you were stamped with a stamp that said, "Good for one salvation only." If you were to lose that salvation, Jesus would have to die again for you to be saved again. You're saved as many times as Jesus died. "For by *one* offering He has perfected forever."

Now somebody may say, "Well, what if I sin after I am saved?" We've all sinned since we've been saved. Jesus is a Savior, not a probation officer. If I depend on my behavior to keep me saved, then I'll be hopelessly lost. If you were to follow me around, you might say, "Oh, he doesn't sin." But you'd make a mistake. I don't steal, I don't commit adultery, I don't use God's name in vain, I don't tell lies. But do you know how the Bible defines sin? The Bible says, "To him who knows to do good and does not do it, to him it is sin" (James 4:17). I don't always do everything I know I ought to do. The Bible says, "The thought of foolishness is sin" (Prov. 24:9 KJV).

56

The Bible says, "Whatsoever is not of faith is sin" (Rom. 14:23 KJV). Do I have perfect faith about everything? No, I'm sad to say.

I wouldn't trust the best fifteen minutes I ever lived to get me to heaven, much less some of my bad ones. And so if I have to depend on my behavior to get me to heaven, I'm not going to make it, and you're not going to make it, and no one is going to make it.

Let me show you a wonderful Scripture, Romans 4:5: "But to him who does not work but believes on Him who justifies the ungodly, his faith is accounted for righteousness." God doesn't say that I'm righteous because of my good works but because I put my faith where God put my sins—on Jesus. Notice what follows: "Just as David also describes the blessedness of the man to whom God imputes righteousness apart from works." Do you know what the word *impute* means? It means to put on one's account. When somebody has something added to their account in Bible terms, it's imputed to them. The next time you go to the department store to buy something, if you want to have a little fun with the clerk, don't say, "Charge it," just say, "Impute it." It means the same thing: "Put that on my account."

When you got saved, God wrote "righteous" on your account. You didn't earn it. Blessed is "the man to whom God imputes righteousness apart from works." God put it on your account apart from your good deeds.

It gets even sweeter. Verse 7 says, "Blessed are those whose lawless deeds are forgiven, and whose sins are covered." Now, watch this: we put our faith in Christ; God calls us righteous. He puts that righteousness on our account without any works of our own, and then it says, "Blessed are those whose lawless deeds are forgiven." That's great!

If you stole ten dollars from me, and you came up to me and said, "I'm sorry, I stole ten dollars from you. Here's the ten dollars," and then you say, "Will you forgive me?" I may say, "Sure, I'll forgive you," but I couldn't cleanse you. You still stole it. All I can do is forgive you. But this Scripture says, "Whose lawless deeds are forgiven, and whose sins are covered." *Covered* means they're blotted out as if it never happened.

But it even gets better. Look at verse 8: "Blessed is the man [now here's the shouting part] to whom the LORD shall not impute sin." Not only does He impute righteousness, not only does He forgive, not only does He blot out my sins, but also the Scripture says, "The LORD shall not impute sin." If God were to put one-half of one sin on my account, I'd be lost forever. If we're depending on ourselves for our security, we'll never have it.

You say, "Well, I did pretty good today, but I did lose my temper in traffic, and I was cross with my child; I did kick the cat. Maybe I won't make it." No, friend, this is a wonderful salvation because it is of God. Now, this is not an excuse to sin, as I'm going to show you later in chapter 4, "What Happens When a Christian Sins."

Remember Calvary's perfect provision. Nobody is saved twice because Jesus died only once, "For by one offering He has perfected *forever* those who are being sanctified" (Heb. 10:14).

The Saint's New Position

What is your new position? When you get saved, it is in Christ Jesus. "Therefore, if anyone is in Christ, he is a new creation; old things have passed away; behold, all things have become new" (2 Cor. 5:17).

There are only two representative persons who've ever lived, and we're all part of one of those two persons—Adam or Christ. In Adam all die. In Christ all are made alive. Everybody is either in Adam or in Christ.

If you're in Christ, that is your new position, and what pertains to Jesus pertains to you. You are in Christ. The only way you could lose your salvation would be for Christ to lose His relationship with the Father because you are in Christ. You are a part of the body of Christ. It is unthinkable that a part of the body of Christ should perish.

A Little "Ark"eology

Because He wants us to understand salvation, God gives many illustrations and object lessons in the Bible. Noah's ark is one of these object lessons of salvation. Peter tells us that the ark is a picture, a type of the Lord Jesus Christ (1 Pet. 3:18–22). I want to see what kind of Bible scholar you are, so I'm going to tell you the story of the ark, and you check me to see if I get it correct.

God said, "Noah, the way people are living is a disgrace, and I'm sorry that I made mankind. I'm going to destroy them with a flood, so, Noah, you build this ark. I'll give you the dimensions; I'll show you how to build it. And after you've gotten it built, Noah, I want you to put some pegs on the side of that ark for you to hold on to. Put eight pegs there—one for yourself and one for Mrs. Noah, one for Shem, one for Ham, one for Japheth, and one for their wives.

"And when the flood starts, Noah, you get a stepladder, get up there and get hold of one of those pegs. And hold on with all your might because it's going to be a rough ride. And Noah, if you can hold on until the water goes down, you'll be safe."

And Noah got hold of one of those little slimy pegs and began to hold on. He looked over to his wife and said, "Sweetheart, you pray for me, that I'll hold out faithful to the end."

Is that the way it happened? Of course not. You know that's not the way it happened. God told Noah to make the ark, and the Bible says, "Then LORD said to Noah, 'Come into the ark.'" He didn't say, "Go into the ark." He said, "Come into the ark" (Gen. 7:1).

If I'm *here* and I say, "You go *there*," that means you go where I'm not. If I'm *here* and say, "Come in *here*," that means you come where I am. Right? So God was in the ark. Had the ark gone down, God would have gone down. And then the Bible says, "And the LORD shut him in" (Gen. 7:16). Why did God shut the door? Two reasons—to shut the water out and to shut Noah in.

Noah and his family were in the ark. How safe was Noah? As safe as the ark. How safe am I? As safe as Jesus, who is my ark of safety. Noah may have fallen down inside the ark, but he never fell out of the ark because God *shut* him in, and God *sealed* him in!

The Bible says in the book of Ephesians that after we're saved, we are "sealed with the Holy Spirit of promise" (Eph. 1:13). We're sealed into the Lord Jesus Christ.

Hallelujah, I Made It!

A lot of folks believe in eternal security, but here's the kind of eternal security they believe in. They say, "Well, one of these days I'm going to get to heaven and say, 'I made it! Hallelujah! Here I am in heaven. Thank God I'm secure.' I'll slam the door behind me. I am safe in heaven." Well now, wait a minute. What makes you think you'll be secure in heaven? The angels fell from heaven. If you're not secure down here, you wouldn't be secure up there.

Security is not in a *place*; it's in a *person*. His name is Jesus! You are *in Christ*. Remember again God's promise in 2 Corinthians 5:17: "If anyone is in Christ, he is a new creation." So that's another reason you can know you are eternally secure—your position in Christ.

The Believer's Eternal Provision

In John 5:24 (KJV) Jesus is speaking, and here is the preface to what He says: "Verily, verily [now when Jesus says, 'Verily, verily,' it means 'Pay attention, pay attention; listen, listen'], I say unto you, He that heareth my word, and believeth on him that sent me, hath everlasting life, and shall not come into condemnation; but is passed from death unto life." Jesus said, "Listen, listen; pay attention. When you hear My word and believe on the God that sent Me to be the Savior of the world, you have everlasting life. You will not come into condemnation, you will not be judged, but you have already passed from death to life."

Question: When do you get eternal life? Do you get eternal life when you die and go to heaven? No! Sometimes you see a grave marker "Entered into Eternal Life." No, friend, if you don't have eternal life before you die, you're not going to get it when they put you in the ground. You get eternal life the moment you believe in Jesus Christ. That's what this Scripture says: "Verily, verily, I say unto you, he that heareth my word, and believeth on him that sent me, *hath* everlasting life [not *will* get], and shall not come into condemnation; but *is* passed from death unto life." Notice it says "*is* passed," not "*will* pass."

Do *you* have everlasting life? If you believe in Christ, you do. When did you get it? When you believed.

If you have everlasting life, will it ever end? Of course not, because it's everlasting. If it ends, whatever you had wasn't everlasting. Suppose you were a Christian for ten years and then you lost your salvation. What did you have? A ten-year life. Suppose you were a Christian for fifty years and then lost it, what did you have? A fifty-year life. Friend, whatever it is that you have, if you ever lose it, whatever it was, it wasn't everlasting.

Jesus said, "I give them everlasting life," not that they will get it when they die. It is present tense. You have everlasting life now. Isn't that great? Sure, it's great; it's wonderful!

Jesus' Interceding Prayer

Jesus is praying for you. His high priestly prayer is in John 17:9. He was praying for His disciples, and here's what He prayed: "I pray for them. I do not pray for the world but for those whom You have given Me, for they are Yours." Jesus was praying for His apostles, for His disciples. What did He pray for them? "I do not pray that You should take them out of the world, but that You should keep them from the evil one" (John 17:15). He says, "Now Lord, I'm not asking that You take them immediately to heaven, but Father I pray that You'll keep them from the evil one."

In Luke 22 when Jesus said to Simon Peter, "Simon, Simon! Indeed, Satan has asked for you, that he may sift you as wheat. But I have prayed for you, that your faith should not fail" (vv. 31–32). Now, did Jesus ever pray a prayer that was not answered? Of course not! He said, "Father, I thank You that . . . You *always* hear Me" (John 11:41). Why? He always prayed to do the will of the Father; He always prayed in faith; sin never inhibited his prayer. Every prayer that He prayed was answered, and He prayed for these disciples, "Father, I pray that You will keep them."

He said, "Peter, the devil wants to sift you like wheat. I'm going to allow him to do it because you need to understand what's in your heart. You need to understand something that needs to be sifted out. I'm going to allow him to do it, but I have prayed for you that your faith won't fail." And that same Peter who cursed and swore and denied Christ was the flaming apostle of Pentecost, who wrote two books in the New Testament because Jesus prayed for him.

You may say, "Yes, sure, Peter was prayed for, and James and Matthew and the rest of them, but Jesus never prayed for me like that." Well, in this same chapter, John 17:20, He says this: "I do not pray for these alone, but also for those who will believe in Me through their word." Just write your name down right there because He might as well have put your name there. Jesus has prayed that you're going to be kept. It was a prayer that transcends the centuries with a delayed detonation.

If He has prayed for you, will His prayer be answered? Absolutely! As a matter of fact, Hebrews 7:25 says, "Therefore He is also able to save to the uttermost those who come to God through Him, since He always lives to make intercession for them." "To save to the uttermost"—do you know what that means? To save all the way—to save you to the end because He's always making intercession for you. The finished work of Jesus is Calvary. He died on the cross and said, "It is finished." But the unfinished work is intercession. He is praying for you and for me, and that prayer is answered. He said, "Father, I thank You that You always hear Me."

God's Almighty Power

I have children and grandchildren, and I want to tell you this: If someone wanted to harm them and somebody wanted to snatch them away from their family, away from love, and destroy them, if I could, I would keep it from happening. Does that make sense to you? If I could, I would keep it from happening.

I'm only human. I don't have all power, but God is able to do it, and He has the power. "Blessed be the God and Father of our Lord Jesus Christ, who according to His abundant mercy has begotten us again to a living hope through the resurrection of Jesus Christ from the dead, to an inheritance incorruptible and undefiled that does not fade away, reserved in heaven for you" (1 Pet. 1:3–4).

Friend, there's a treasure laid up in glory for you, and the lawyers can't get it, inflation can't touch it, the gnawing tooth of time and the foul breath of decay can't destroy it. It's there; that's your inheritance, but the next verse says, "For you, who are kept by the power of God." You're kept by the power of God. It's not a matter of your holding onto Him; it's a matter of Him holding onto you.

People say, "Just pray for me that I'll hold out faithful to the end." Well, we should pray for one another that we'll be faithful Christians, but it's not our holding out, it's Him holding us. Jesus said, "Neither shall anyone snatch them out of My hand. My Father, who has given them to Me, is greater than all; and no one is able to snatch them out of My Father's hand" (John 10:28–29).

Can you imagine a power that is strong enough to pry open the hand of God and take you out? Some people say, "I think the devil could take you away from God." Oh, you do? You think the devil can take you away? Well, then, if he could, why hasn't he? Think about it. Hasn't the devil been nice to you? He has the power, but he just hasn't done it. Now that's a strange doctrine, isn't it? You're going to heaven by the goodness of the devil. No, no, no! You're going to heaven by the grace of God, and the only reason the devil hasn't taken you out of the hand of God is he can't.

"My sheep hear My voice, and I know them, and they follow Me. And I give them eternal life, and . . . [no one is able to] snatch them out of My hand" (John 10:27–29). Friend, we're kept by the power of God.

Don't ever get the idea that because you're eternally secure, it makes no difference how you live. God will cure that theory in a hurry because God will carry you to the woodshed. "For whom the LORD loves He chastens" (Heb. 12:6). Don't get the idea this is a license to sin—that's foolish.

I Sin All I Want To

Some people say, "If I believe in eternal security, I can just get saved and sin all I want to." I sin all I want to. I sin *more* than I want to. I don't want to. Nothing would please me better than to know I'd never sin again. One of these days, when God is finished with me, I will never sin again, but I'd just as soon eat dirt as to willingly sin. And if you still want to, you need to get your "wanter" fixed; you need to be born again. "If any one is in Christ, he is a new creation; old things have passed away; behold all things have become new."

I've given you eight reasons, straight from the Bible, that you can know that you are eternally secure. Remember, it's great to be saved. It's even better to be saved and know you're saved. And it is even more wonderful that you can be saved, know that you are saved, and know that you can never lose it.

Every Christian Ought to Know

WHAT HAPPENS WHEN A CHRISTIAN SINS

Have mercy upon me, O God,
According to Your lovingkindness;
According to the multitude of Your tender mercies,
Blot out my transgressions.
Wash me thoroughly from my iniquity, and cleanse
me from my sin.

PSALM 51:1–2

What happens when a Christian sins? If we can't lose our salvation, does that mean we have nothing to lose when we sin?

I heard a story a while back about a former prizefighter. He had been converted, and he thought God had called him to preach. The only problem was, while he thought he had the gift of preaching, nobody else had the gift of listening, so he couldn't get a church. He got a little pulpit, found a street corner, and preached to passersby in Chicago. He had two or three hangers-on, friends that liked him; he had two or three that hated him; and he had one man, a professed atheist, who said, "I don't believe any of the Bible." These two, the ex-prizefighter and the so-called atheist, who was a pseudo intellectual, would get into arguments.

One day the former prizefighter was ready for him. He said to the atheist, "Listen, if I can prove to you just one verse in the Bible is true, will you apologize to me?" And this so-called atheist said, "Yes, indeed I would." With that the former prizefighter reached out and took this man by the nose and twisted it so severely that the blood ran down both nostrils; and then with a smile on his face, he opened the Bible and read Proverbs 30:33: "The churning of milk produces butter, and wringing the nose produces blood." Then he said, "I want you to apologize to me because I proved to you at least one verse in the Bible is true."

Just as surely as the churning of milk brings forth butter, and just as surely as the wringing of the nose brings forth blood, if you are bound to sin, you are bound to suffer—whether you are saved or whether you are lost.

In Psalm 51, we find the story of King David's sin. David committed a horrible, heinous, hurtful sin, yet he was a child of God. I expect to meet David in heaven. He was a man after God's own heart, and yet he committed awful, terrible, horrible sin. What we see is this—if a person is bound to *sin,* he is bound to *suffer.* He will not lose his salvation, but suffering follows sin as night follows day.

Consider first of all the consequences of sin in the life of a Christian, and then think about the cleansing of sin in the life of a Christian.

Remember that Psalm 51 was written by David after he had gotten his heart right with God. He's looking back on the consequences of sin in his life, and he writes this story, this record for us to read and learn from. You may want to get a Bible and keep it open to Psalm 51 as we continue.

Consequences of Sin in the Life of a Christian

Sin Dirties the Soul

Here David is praying, "O God, wash me; O God, cleanse me." Now, he's a king; he dresses in his royal robes; he sleeps on his silken bed; he bathes in his marble tub with his perfumed soap; yet he feels grimy; he feels dirty.

Did you know that if you're a child of God and you sin, spiritually you're going to feel dirty? And if you don't feel dirty when you sin, you need to ask yourself if you've ever been saved. No pig has ever said, "Woe is me, I'm dirty." A pig has no concept of being dirty because that is his element. The child of God realizes that he is dirty when he sins.

A lot of people have a form of religion, but they've never been cleansed to begin with. They've been starched and ironed, but they've never been washed. They have this dirt that's there all the time, so they never really feel dirty. But a true child of God, when he sins, feels unclean. And if you're a child of God and you've sinned, you have felt that. I want to say this: If you can sin and don't feel dirty and grimy, spiritually you need to ask yourself: "Have I ever been saved? Do I really know the Lord?"

Sin Dominates the Mind

In verse 3, David says, "For I acknowledge my transgressions, and my sin is always before me." Think about that: "My sin is always before me." Day and night, night and day, what David had done had so etched itself upon his consciousness, so reverberated through his spirit, that he was conscious of it all the time.

A test as to whether you're saved is not if you can sin but if you can sin and just ignore it, forget it. If you're a child of God, the Holy Spirit will not let you ignore it; He will not let you forget it. The Holy Spirit will put His finger on the sore spot and push. David said, "My sin is always before me." It dominated his mind. Now that doesn't mean that he was necessarily consciously thinking of it all day long.

There may be sin in your heart and in your life. And maybe you're trying to work out a mathematical problem, and you're not thinking at that precise moment about that sin, but that doesn't mean that your sin is not always there. It is there either in your conscious mind or, perhaps worse, in your subconscious mind. You may kick it out the front door, but it will run around the house and come in the basement window. It will show up in your subconscious as an irritable temper, the inability to concentrate, sleepless nights, lack of joy. Your sin is there night and day. If you can just sin and forget it, you need to ask yourself, "Have I ever really been saved?"

There are two kinds of wounds that can come to the human soul, the human psyche. One is guilt and the other is sorrow. Sorrow is a clean wound. Give it time; it will heal, but guilt is a dirty wound. It just festers and festers and festers and never stops until it is cleansed.

And so here is David, praying, "O God, my soul feels dirty; my mind is dominated by this thing that I have done."

Sin Disgraces the Lord

In verse 4, David is speaking to God: "Against You, You only, have I sinned, and done this evil in Your sight—that You may be found just when You speak, and blameless when You judge." Think about the first part of that verse. He says, "Against You, You only, have I sinned." Now against whom did David sin?

When you think about it, you might say, "Well, he committed adultery, so he sinned against his own body. He certainly committed sin against his wife when he committed adultery. And not only did he sin against his body and his wife, but he also sinned against his children and his family. Moreover, he sinned against the nation." None of these is mentioned. He saw sin for what it actually was—an affront to Almighty God!

David loved God. That's the reason David's heart was broken. He said, "O God, against You, You only, have I sinned and done this evil in Your sight." When people want to commit adultery, sometimes they go off to some secret rendezvous, some secret liaison, some hidden place. But it dawned on David, "My God, You were watching me. Your eyes saw what I did. O God, my God, God, the God that I love, Lord, I have sinned against You. Not only have I broken Your law, but I have broken Your heart."

An unsaved man sometimes feels bad about what his sin does to him. A saved man feels bad about what his sin does to God. That's the difference. When a slave disobeys, what's he afraid of? The whip. But a son, when he disobeys, is hurt because of his father's displeasure. When you love the Lord God, you can know that you're saved when it's not the punishment but the sin that stings your conscience.

David said, "God, not only has my sin dirtied my soul, not only does it dominate my mind, it has disgraced my God! God, I have sinned against You."

Sin Depresses the Heart

Look in verse 8 of this psalm. He's talking about the consequences of his sin, and he says, "Make me hear joy and gladness, that the bones You have broken may rejoice." He's depressed; there's no joy, no gladness. Oh, it seemed thrilling while he was doing it, while he was committing the sin. For the Bible says, "Bread gained by deceit is sweet to a man, but afterward his mouth will be filled with gravel" (Prov. 20:17). David has lost his joy. Look in verse 12: "Restore to me the *joy* of Your salvation." He's not saying, "Lord, restore my salvation." He had his salvation, but he had lost the joy of his salvation.

The most miserable person on earth is not a lost person; the most miserable person on earth is a saved person out of fellowship with God. Only one thing can take the joy from your heart—not two, not three, not four—just one, and it is sin. And only one kind of sin— *yours*. When someone sins against you, that is *their* sin. Your reaction to what they do to you can take away your joy. If you were to slap me in the face, that could not take the joy out of my heart. It may hurt, and it could take my happiness, but it couldn't take my joy.

It could take your joy, but it couldn't take mine. If I react to you in the wrong way, then that will take my joy.

By the way, if you want to see what I am or what any person is, don't watch their actions, watch their reactions because their reactions are what they really are. Slapping me in the face only gives you an opportunity to see my reaction. If you want to see what a person is full of, just see what spills out when they're jostled. If you jostle somebody and anger spills out, they're full of anger. If you jostle somebody and Jesus spills out, they're full of Jesus. If you want to know what I really am, watch when somebody steals my parking place or cuts me off on the expressway and see how I react—then you'll know the real person.

What I am saying is that joy is to be constant no matter what anybody else does. Now you say, "Well, wait a minute, I'm not supposed to be happy all the time." I agree with you, you're not supposed to be happy all the time. I'm not talking about happiness; I'm talking about *joy*.

There's a difference between happiness and joy. Happiness depends on what happens; that's why we call it happiness. If your "hap" is good, you're happy; if your "hap" is bad, you're unhappy; and sometimes we have bad "haps." We're not supposed to be happy all the time.

You wouldn't want to be happy all of the time. You'd get sick and tired of being happy all of the time. You don't have to go around with a goony grin on your face all the time. To be happy all the time would be like having ice cream for every meal.

Jesus was a man of sorrows; Jesus wept. He was not happy all the time, but he *was* full of joy. While facing the cross, Jesus spoke to His disciples and said, "These things I have spoken to You, that My joy may remain in you, and that your joy may be full" (John 15:11). When He was facing cruel Calvary, He was speaking of joy. Is it any wonder Paul could write from a dismal prison this injunction?— "Rejoice in the Lord always" (Phil. 4:4).

The joy of the Lord is constant, and the joy of the Lord is your strength. Happiness is like a thermometer; it registers conditions. Joy is like a thermostat; it controls conditions.

Something really wonderful is when you get happiness and joy, when they just come together. Those are wonderful times. Maybe you're having a wonderful holiday season, your family is there, and you're having a lot of fun. When you're with other Christians who love the Lord and are praying for one another, the joy of Jesus is there. That's wonderful, when happiness and joy come together.

When happiness is gone, joy becomes all the more important. And sometimes God gives you joy, not to take away the pain but to help you bear it. And in the midst of excruciating pain, there can be supernatural joy. Barbara Johnson puts it this way: "Pain is inevitable, but misery is optional."

Sin Diseases the Body

Sin in your life, without repentance, can actually make your body sick. Notice again in verse 8: "Make me hear joy and gladness, that the bones You have broken may rejoice." Now remember this is poetry. David didn't have any compound fractures, but he's talking about his bones being broken. He's using a figure of speech. We do the same thing today. Did you ever say, "I was just crushed." Well, what does that mean? It doesn't mean that somebody put you into a trash compactor. But it does mean that you are being squeezed in; there's pressure on you. And David is saying, "God, You are squeezing the life out of me. Make me hear joy and gladness that the bones You have broken may rejoice."

Sometimes we have the idea that if we sin, God is just going to toss us off. Oh no, He doesn't toss us off; He squeezes all the tighter. He had the pressure on David, and David was saying, "God, You're squeezing the life out of me." That's one of the ways he could know that he was saved: God would not let him go. God just squeezed him all the tighter because of the sin that was in his life.

How long can someone have that pressure on his life before it affects his body? You see, the Bible says, "A merry heart does good, like medicine, but a broken spirit dries the bones" (Prov. 17:22). In the same way joy works like medicine, misery works like a poison.

Here David is under this incredible pressure. When a person gets under psychological and spiritual pressure, it may affect the body. We call that "psychosomatic illness." *Psycho* means "mind"; *soma* means "body." The mind makes the body sick. And we all know that, even in just very common ways.

Has Anyone Seen the Pepto-Bismol?

Let me give you an illustration. Mother calls that dinner is ready, and so father, mother, sister, and brother sit down to this wonderful meal that mother has fixed. Everything is fine until brother asks, "Dad, can I use the car tonight?" and sister says, "No, you can't use the car tonight. You used the car last night. It's my night to use the car." And brother says to sister, "You shut up. I wasn't talking to you. I was talking to Dad." And Dad says, "Don't you use the words *shut up*. We don't speak that way in our house." And then brother says, "Well, she started it," and he says, "Listen, you kids, I said, 'Shut up!'" and mother says, "You just told him not to say, 'Shut up.'" He says, "You shut up!" And then brother and sister and father and mother are, just like that, into an argument. The dinner is getting cold. Finally they eat a few bites, everybody gets up and goes off somewhere; and about thirty minutes later somebody says, "Has anybody seen the Pepto-Bismol?" What has happened? You know exactly what has happened: our bodies have reacted to our hearts, our minds, our spirits.

I was reading that a mother who gets into fits of temper can even cause her baby who is nursing at her breast to become colicky. You know, we're just a unit; we're all tied together. And when we read other psalms, it seems like David actually was physically ill, and I believe it was a direct result of his sin.

In 1 Corinthians 11:30, Paul scolded the Corinthians for acting irreverently at the Lord's table. He said, "For this reason many are weak and sick among you, and many sleep." He meant they were dead because of the sin that was in their life.

Sin sickens the body. A merry heart, the joy of the Lord, is a wonderful medicine. The Bible says, "The joy of the Lord is your strength" (Neh. 8:10). When you're happy in Jesus, you sleep better. When there's joy, you digest your food, your juices flow, your glands secrete as they ought to because there's joy in the Lord.

Sin Defiles the Spirit

Next, sin defiles the spirit. In verse 10, David says, "Create in me a clean heart, O God, and renew a steadfast spirit within me." David had a sour spirit. David had a defiled spirit.

I'm going to make a confession to you. If I had my choice for company, I'd rather be around a sinner who has never been saved, just for company, than a saved person out of fellowship with God.

Folks who are saved but out of fellowship are cantankerous and vituperative and hard to get along with. Some of the most irritating people you ever see are Christians who are out of joint spiritually. They get a sour spirit, and nothing will please them. You know, no dish on the table looks good if you have dyspepsia. And there's nothing that can please these kinds of people. You can tell when a person is backsliding. In a church they begin to get a critical spirit.

In any church there is plenty in everybody and everything to criticize, if that's what you focus on—just look around. When people are backsliding, they take their eyes off the Lord, and then they begin to put their eyes on the faults of those for whom Jesus died.

And David, as you'll see, had a critical spirit; he had a defiled spirit. Let me illustrate what I'm talking about. Nathan the prophet, who was like David's pastor, came to call. Now remember, David had committed adultery. And then in order to cover his adultery, he had Uriah the Hittite, Bathsheba's husband, slain in battle to try to cover the sin.

Nathan knew it, and he came before the king and said, "King, there's a matter that you need to adjudicate; there's a matter that you need to judge." He said, "King, in the kingdom is a man who has everything his heart could desire—houses, lands, flocks, herds, big family. He lives next door to a man that had nothing except one little pet lamb. It was like one of his own children, ate from his own table." And he said, "David, this man that was very rich had a stranger to come by, just dropped in for a visit, and the rich man went over here and took the poor man's lamb, his little pet lamb, killed it and barbecued it and fed it to that stranger. David, what do you think ought to be done to that man?"

David was livid. He jumped up on the throne. He said, "The man that has done that will pay fourfold." Nathan said, "And you're the man!" Nathan had created a parable to show David how defiled his spirit had become.

Notice how quickly David judged this other man. He judged the man for stealing a lamb; he had stolen a woman. He judged somebody for killing an animal; he had killed a man. He, with a cross tie in his own eye, was going to try to pick a speck out of somebody else's eye. The backslider is always that way; he always has a sour spirit, a vile spirit, finding fault in everybody else.

I heard a story years ago about a man in a particular church. It was a small church, and all small churches have self-styled watchdogs. These are people who think they're God's appointed and anointed to make sure everything goes right in their church. This man opened the door to a broom closet, and there were five brand new brooms. He went to see the church treasurer and asked, "Why have we spent all this money on five brooms? We are not meeting our budget, and there are five brooms in that broom closet."

The treasurer couldn't pacify him, and he ended up talking to the pastor. And the pastor said, "Well, brother, I don't know. Maybe there was a sale on brooms; maybe we use a lot of brooms, but it's only five brooms. Don't fall out of fellowship over five brooms."

Later on, however, the treasurer was having coffee with the pastor, and he said, "Pastor, that's easy to understand. How would you feel if you saw everything you had given to the church in the past year tied up in five brooms?"

Folks who are out of fellowship with God are quick to find fault with other people. If you want to, you can always find fault because all of us are just a society of sinners who finally realized it and banded ourselves together to do something about it.

Sin Destroys the Testimony

So here's David, a man after God's own heart. He loves God, but he has gotten into horrible, terrible sin. Not only does it defile the spirit, but it destroys the testimony. This may be one of the worst things about sin in the life of a child of God. Notice Psalm 51:14: "Deliver me from the guilt of bloodshed, O God, the God of my salvation, and my tongue shall sing aloud of Your righteousness."

Do you know why people don't sing in the worship service? They're not filled with the Spirit. They're just filled with sin. They've got nothing to sing about. They've lost their song because they have lost their testimony.

Look at verse 15: "O Lord, open my lips, and my mouth shall show forth Your praise." He's not praising God; his lips are sealed. His sin has destroyed his testimony, and praise has dried up. He's not bringing souls to Christ because he says in verses 12–13: "Restore to me the joy of Your salvation, and uphold me by Your generous Spirit. *Then* I will teach transgressors Your ways, and sinners shall be converted to You." Do you see what happened? No praise, no song, no soul-winning. Why? I'll tell you why: sin had destroyed his testimony.

Sometimes in church you will see people who just sit there with their arms folded, who seem to say, "Bless me if you can." And why aren't they praising God? Why aren't they fellowshipping? Why aren't they happy? Why can't they say, "Glory to God"? Why can't they lift their hearts to Jesus in praise? Something inside is not right.

Andrew Murray said there are two classes of Christians—soul-winners and backsliders. Manley Beasley used to say, "You get right with God, you will have to backslide to keep from winning souls."

What are the consequences of sin in the life of a Christian? It dirties the soul; it dominates the mind; it disgraces the Lord; it depresses the heart; it diseases the body; it defiles the spirit; and it destroys the testimony.

Can a Christian sin? Yes. Can a Christian sin and not suffer? No. Remember, the most miserable man on Earth is not an unsaved man but a saved man out of fellowship with God.

Cleansing of Sin in the Life of a Christian

Let's just turn the psalm over and look at it from another viewpoint and think about the cleansing of sin in the life of a Christian. I want to give you four steps that will show you how to bring the song back, how to bring back the joy, how to get right with God.

Confidence

Notice Psalm 51:1: "Have mercy upon me, O God, according to Your lovingkindness; according to the multitude of Your tender mercies, blot out my transgressions." Do you know what David knew? David knew for a multitude of sins, there were a multitude of mercies. David knew that God had not stopped loving him. He says, "According to Your lovingkindness." God does not love us because we're valuable; we are valuable because He loves us. God does not love us because we're good. "God demonstrates His own love toward us, in that while we were still sinners, Christ died for us" (Rom. 5:8). We need to have this confidence that no matter what we have done, God loves us.

Never tell a child who is tempted to do wrong, "Now, if you do that, God won't love you anymore." That's a lie. There's nothing you can do to make Him love you any more; there's nothing you can do to make Him love you any less. He loves you. Your sin may break His heart, but He loves you. If we could only understand that God does love us, and for a *multitude of sins there is a multitude of mercies.*

Blessed Dogs

A man put the following ad in the Lost and Found section of the paper: "LOST DOG. Crippled in front paw, blind in left eye, mange on back and neck, tail missing. Recently neutered. Answers to the name Lucky." And he was a lucky dog. I'll tell you why he was a lucky dog. In spite of all of the stuff that was wrong with him, somebody loved him enough to want him.

You know, we're lucky dogs; better, we're blessed dogs. God loves us out of sheer grace. And I want you to have this confidence: God loves you with an everlasting love. That's the sheer grace of God. When we understand this, we say, "O to grace, how great a debtor. Daily I'm constrained to be."[1]

God loves you. Marvel of marvels, wonder of wonders! Even though David had committed a horrible, hurtful, heinous sin, he could have the confidence to pray, "O God, according to Your loving-kindness; according to the multitude of Your tender mercies."

Confession

Psalm 51:2–3: "Wash me thoroughly from my iniquity, and cleanse me from my sin. For *I acknowledge my transgressions,* and, my sin is always before me." Notice what David calls it—"my sin," not somebody else's. He is saying: "God, *I* am the sinner; God, *I* am the one that has sinned. I acknowledge my sin. My sin, my transgression." As the old spiritual says, "It's not my brother, not my sister, but it's me, O Lord, standing in the need of prayer." There's one thing that God will never accept for sin, and that is an alibi. *Jesus did not die for alibis, Jesus died for sin.*

Not Just an Admission

The Bible says in 1 John 1:9, "If we confess our sins, He is faithful and just to forgive us our sins and to cleanse us from all unrighteousness." And that word *"confess"* as used in the New Testament is made up of two words: *homos* and *lego,* which means "to say the same thing." To admit your sin is not to confess your sin in the Bible sense. You may admit your sin in a courtroom, but a confession of sin means to say the same as God says. God says, "This is wrong, Adrian. You have done wrong; you have sinned." And I say, "Yes, God, I agree with you. I come over on your side, and I say about that sin what you say about that sin. God, I agree with you; I confess my sin."

People have always wanted to make excuses for their sin. It began in the Garden of Eden; do you remember? "Adam, where are you? Have you done this?" "Well, Lord, it really wasn't my fault. It was the woman you gave me; it was her fault." And God spoke to Eve, and Eve said, "Well, Lord, you know the serpent beguiled me." Of course the snake didn't have a leg to stand on!

Human nature wants to say, "It's not me; it's somebody else." The excuses abound: I was raised in a dysfunctional family. My mother wouldn't let me push the mush off the highchair when I was a kid. Temper runs in my family. I had a glandular malfunction. Whatever it is, it is some kind of an alibi rather than a confession. Friend, that confidence has to be followed by a confession: "I acknowledge my transgression."

The Bible teaches, "He who covers his sins will not prosper, but whoever confesses and forsakes them will have mercy" (Prov. 28:13). When we try to cover it, God uncovers it. When we uncover it, God covers it. "If we confess our sins, He is faithful and just to forgive us our sins and to cleanse us from all unrighteousness" (1 John 1:9). And friend, you and I *can* be perfectly, totally clean.

The Difference between Accusation and Conviction

You need to learn the difference between satanic accusation and Holy Spirit conviction. The devil is the accuser of the brethren. He will do this in two ways:

1. The devil will accuse you about sin that has already been confessed. He will try to dig it up again. Friend, when God buries it, it is gone. He will never bring you into double jeopardy. He is "faithful and just to forgive us our sins and to cleanse us from all unrighteousness" (1 John 1:9), and, "Do not call anything impure that God has made clean" (Acts 11:9 NIV). "The blood of Jesus Christ . . . cleanses us from all sin" (1 John 1:7).

But the devil will sometimes accuse you about things you did years ago. You've put it under the blood and been forgiven, but he just keeps dredging it up.

2. The devil will try to make you feel guilty for no reason. You just kind of feel bad all over. So you end up praying this way, "O God, if I have sinned, forgive me." Friend, do away with that kind of prayer. That's not the kind of prayer David prayed. The Bible says, "If we confess our sins." Name that sin! That's the only way you'll know that you're really forgiven. Just call it by name.

But the devil will either try to dredge up sin that has already been forgiven or to make you feel bad about something without giving it a name. That is *accusation.*

What is *conviction*? Conviction is the Holy Spirit saying, "This and this and this you have done," and like a good doctor, He'll put his finger right on the sore spot, and He will push. He will call it by name and want you to confess it and be cleansed. And that's so wonderful. Don't let the devil accuse you of sin that's been forgiven or accuse you of things that have never been committed. The Holy Spirit of God will convict you specifically, and then you confess it, and you can be clean.

Cleansing

Sin makes you feel dirty, so God just gives you a spiritual bath. In verse 2, David says, "Wash me." This speaks of being outwardly cleansed because sin is defilement. Then, in verse 7 he says, "Purge me." This speaks of cleansing on the inside. "Be of sin the double cure, save from wrath and make me pure."[2] You *can* be as pure as the driven snow. "If we confess our sins, He is faithful and just to forgive us our sins and to cleanse us from all unrighteousness" (1 John 1:9). "Though your sins are like scarlet, they shall be as white as snow; though they are red like crimson, they shall be as wool" (Isa. 1:18). It is the cleansing power of the grace of God.

You don't have to carry that baggage around. God cleanses. Now you probably have not gotten into the industrial-strength sin that David did, but he was cleansed, and you can be clean.

A pastor friend of mine and his wife were out celebrating their anniversary, and they passed a dress shop. It was one of those kinds of dress shop chains that the pastor's wife wouldn't normally go in because the dresses were very expensive. There in the window was a beautiful white dress, and it seemed just right for her. And just for recreation, they went in to see it, and he said, "Sweetheart, try it on," and she put it on. It didn't have to be altered; it was perfect. It was her fit; it flattered her; it made her look gorgeous. They looked at the price tag and gulped, but he said to her, "Darling, it's our anniversary. I'm going to buy you that dress." and he bought it.

Later they were having dinner. They were sitting there; she was dressed in that dress, and they had cherry pie for dessert. It happened—in her lap, a piece of cherry pie on that white dress. The next scene was the dry cleaners. They brought that dress in and asked the owner, "Can you remove this stain?" He said, "Well, what is it?" And she said, "It's cherry." "Oh lady, on a white dress, I don't think so. Maybe—I won't promise. Just leave it, I'll do the best I can."

They went away, and they came back, and she asked the question that she was afraid to ask, "Did you get the stain out?" And he said, "Well, let me show you. If you look at it carefully, you can see there's been a stain there, but the average person would never, ever see it." They paid him and took the dress home. She never wore it again because she knew that stain was there. That's a sad story, isn't it?

Let me give you a story with a happy ending. There is no stain the blood of Jesus cannot remove—none! "The blood of Jesus Christ His Son cleanses us from all sin" (1 John 1:7). David says, "Purge me . . . and I shall be clean; wash me and I shall be whiter than snow" (Ps. 51:7).

Consecration

In Psalm 51:12–15, David says, "Restore to me the joy of Your salvation, and uphold me by Your generous Spirit. Then I will teach transgressors Your ways, and sinners shall be converted to You. Deliver me from the guilt of bloodshed, O God, the God of my salvation, and my tongue shall sing aloud of Your righteousness. O Lord, open my lips, and my mouth shall show forth Your praise." He is saying, "Lord, put my feet on the right path, and God, I am going to get back to serving You." God doesn't just cleanse us just so we can sit around and be clean; He puts us back on the track of service.

Do you know how David got into trouble in the first place? He was not doing what he should have been doing. The Bible says it was the time when kings went to war. And in the evening David rolled up off his bed. That rascal had been in bed all afternoon. He got up, and he looked from the rooftop and saw Bathsheba. An idle mind is the devil's workshop. And that's the reason the sins of omission are greater than the sins of commission.

Did you know that if you're doing what you ought to be doing, you can't be doing what you ought not to be doing? When you sin, once you get your heart clean, get back into service. Remember the four steps of restoration—confidence, confession, cleansing, and consecration.

Don't get the idea that because you can be cleansed it makes no difference whether you sin. Just as surely as you put your hand on a hot stove and get burned, if you sin, you're bound to suffer, but thank God for His wonderful, marvelous, matchless grace that forgives and restores the sinning Christian.

5

Every Christian Ought to Know

HOW TO HANDLE TEMPTATION

Therefore let him who thinks he stands take heed lest he fall. No temptation has overtaken you except such as is common to man; but God is faithful, who will not allow you to be tempted beyond what you are able, but with the temptation will also make the way of escape, that you may be able to bear it.
1 CORINTHIANS 10:12–13

Temptation is all around. We don't have to go looking for it. It finds us. We are not tempted because we are sinful. Jesus was tempted. We are tempted because we are human. Handled rightly, temptations can bring us closer to God. This chapter will tell us how to turn temptations into triumphs.

Three Ways to Handle Temptation

Give In to It

One way is just give in to it. We have a generation today that says, "Who is bothered by temptation? I just do what I want to do." This crowd says, "Whatever is natural is beautiful, and whatever is beautiful must be right, so if it feels good do it." A lot of people are living that way, and that's really on the animal plane. An animal lives for self-propagation, self-preservation, and self-gratification. They are like the lady who said, "I can overcome anything but temptation." They just give in to it.

Fight It

Then there are those who fight temptation in the strength of their flesh. They're always battling temptation—just the opposite of those who give in. Constantly struggling but constantly failing. I think we've all been there—fighting and failing, fighting and failing—like the little boy who was sitting under the farmer's apple tree. The farmer said, "Are you trying to steal an apple?" The boy answered, "No sir, I'm trying *not* to."

I heard of a man on a diet. Doughnuts were a no-no. On the way to work, he had to drive past the doughnut shop. Temptation beckoned to him: "Just think how great a fresh doughnut and a steaming cup of coffee would be." The man said to himself, "I'll stop only if there is a place to park right at the front door." Would you believe it? After circling the block three times, there it was—a parking place right at the front door! Could this be providence?

A lot of times we are like the little boy under the apple tree or the man circling the doughnut shop. We try to fight temptation, but we fail.

Overcome It Through Christ

The way to overcome temptation is to overcome through the Lord Jesus Christ. I want you to cheer up; there is help. Believe it or not, you *can* live victoriously—whether your temptation is in the realm of overeating, whether it's in the area of lust, or whether it's in the area of laziness—whatever it is, you don't have to be a slave to the world, the flesh, and the devil. The Bible says in 1 Corinthians 10:12–13: "Therefore let him who thinks he stands take heed lest he fall. No temptation has overtaken you except such as is common to man; but God is faithful, who will not allow you to be tempted beyond what you are able, but with the temptation will also make the way of escape that you may be able to bear it."

The Subjects of Temptation

Who may be tempted? We all are subject to temptation. Don't get the idea that when you get saved you won't be tempted any more. You *will* be tempted. You will be bombarded with temptations in the areas of dishonesty, materialism, sex, greed, and pride. Being saved does not make you immune to temptation, and being tempted is not a sin. Jesus "was in all points tempted like as we are, yet without sin" (Heb. 4:15 KJV)." But be careful that you guard against pride. Remember what verse 12 says: "Therefore let him who thinks he stands take heed lest he fall." The proud person tempts the devil to tempt him, and if you are cavalier or careless about sin, I can tell you that you are going to fall.

The person that is in the greatest danger, however, is the person who is trying to fight this temptation in the strength of his own flesh. He thinks, *I don't need to read a book on temptation. I don't have any problem with temptation. I can overcome it.* But without Christ you cannot. God has to make a way of escape for you.

Why doesn't God just kill the devil? Why doesn't God just remove all temptation from us? Because that's not God's plan for us. God's plan is not immunity, but victory.

Why Not Play on Thursday Afternoon?

I used to play football. Football is quite a game. Someone takes a bagful of zipped-up air, pointed on each end, and goes out on a cow pasture with ten other companions and says, "We're going to take this bagful of air down to the other end of that cow pasture." Then there are eleven people standing on the opposite side saying, "Oh, no, you're not!" The first team replies, "Oh, yes, we are!" Up and down the field they run, back and forth. That's all it is; it's just a big contest. Finally, when one team puts that bag of air over the line called the goal line and into the end zone, everybody cheers. It's a strenuous game. People beat their brains out over it. There's a lot of strategy and skill in a game of football.

But why do they do that on Saturday afternoon? Why don't they just go out there on Thursday, say about four in the afternoon when the other team is not there, and score on every play? They could just move that ball up and down the field, and every play would be a touchdown! I'll tell you why. There's no glory in that. There's no victory in that. God's plan for us is *victory*. He wants us to triumph in the Lord Jesus Christ.

We're all subject to temptation so that we can learn how to depend on the Lord Jesus Christ and know victory. There is no Christian who does not know temptation. Don't get the idea that if you're a pastor, you're immune to temptation. Don't get the idea that if you're a saint, you won't be tempted. Again, I remind you that Jesus was tempted in all points like as we are (see Heb. 4:15 KJV).

The Source of Temptation

Where does temptation come from? It comes from one of three sources: the world, the flesh, or the devil. That's the unholy trinity of temptation—the world, the flesh, and the devil. Your temptation is not unique. Don't get the idea that you're uniquely tempted and nobody else knows the same kind of temptation that you know. When we're tempted, we're all tempted basically in the same way, either by the world, the flesh, or the devil.

The External Foe—the World

"Do not love the world or the things in the world. If anyone loves the world, the love of the Father is not in him" (1 John 2:15). First, let's think a little bit about the world. I call the world the *external* foe. The world is the enemy out there. When I say the world, I'm not talking about planet Earth. Planet Earth is not evil. God created this world. So when the Bible says, "Love not the world," He's not talking about the planet. Jesus loved nature. Jesus said, "Consider the lilies of the field, how they grow: they neither toil nor spin; and yet I say to you that even Solomon in all his glory was not arrayed like one of these" (Matt. 6:28–29). When God created the natural world, He said, "It is good."

We're not talking about the world of nature; nor are we talking about the world of people when the Bible says "the world." We're not to love the world, but we're to love people. The Bible says, "For God so loved the world [the world of people] that He gave His only begotten Son" (John 3:16). So when He says, "Love not the world," He's not talking about the planet; He's not talking about the people. The world He is talking about is a system. The word that is translated *world* is the Greek word *cosmos,* meaning "a system, an order of things."

"Do not love the world [do not love the cosmos], or the things in the world. If anyone loves the world, the love of the Father is not in him" (1 John 2:15). "And do not be conformed to this world" (Rom. 12:2). "Adulterers and adulteresses! Do you not know that friendship with the world is enmity with God?" (James 4:4). All of these verses use the word *world* in a different sense—not talking about the planet, not talking about the people, but talking about a system, an order of things.

The world doesn't have to be hideous. Sometimes we think of something worldly like a bar or a casino, or some dive somewhere. The world may be very beautiful; the world can be very attractive. You can be molded by some very gorgeous and high-sounding things. It's just an order of things, a system of things that is contrary to our Lord and His ways.

In 1 Peter 3:3, Peter is telling a wife who is saved how to win her unsaved husband to Christ. He tells her how to behave and how to talk, and then he actually tells her how to be truly beautiful. He says, "Do not let your adornment be merely outward—arranging the hair, wearing gold, or putting on fine apparel—rather let it be the hidden person of the heart." And the word *adornment* is the same word that's translated *world* more than one hundred times in the Bible. We could easily paraphrase 1 Peter 3:3 like this: "Do not let your world be the world of the beauty shop, the jeweler, the dressmaker."

Sometimes people read that verse and think, *A woman ought not to wear jewelry; she ought not go to the beautician; she ought not to wear makeup.* This is not an injunction against looking nice. You are not going to win your husband by looking like an unmade bed.

What's Peter saying here? He's not saying it's wrong to fix your hair; he's not saying it's wrong to wear gold. Let's be reasonable. He also says, "Don't let your adornment be the putting on of clothes." If it's wrong to fix your hair, if it's wrong to wear gold, then it's wrong to wear clothes. He's not saying these things are wrong. He's simply saying that is not to be your true beauty. He's saying, "Don't let that be your world!"

And the guys say, "Yeah, tell them!" If he were speaking to men, he might say, "Whose world, let it not be the world of business, let it not be the world of sports." These things are not wrong in themselves, but they can squeeze us into a mold. Whether symbolized by Madison Avenue or Wall Street, if we're not careful, we can embrace this value system the Bible calls the world, the external foe, and can get drawn away from our Lord.

The Internal Foe—the Flesh

"Now the works of the flesh are evident, which are: adultery, fornication, uncleanness, lewdness, idolatry, sorcery, hatred, contentions, jealousies, outbursts of wrath, selfish ambitions, dissensions, heresies, envy, murders, drunkenness, revelries, and the like; of which I tell you beforehand, just as I also told you in time past, that those who practice such things will not inherit the kingdom of God" (Gal. 5:19–21).

When this passage says "flesh," the Bible is not talking about your hide, your hair, your nerves, your corpuscles; it's not talking about physical bodies. Your physical body is not evil. As a matter of fact, Romans 12:1 says you are to present your body to the Lord as a living sacrifice. First Corinthians 6:19 says that "your body is the temple of the Holy Spirit." Your body is not evil. God made your body, and your body is to be given to him as a temple.

The Bible is using the word *flesh* to mean the predisposition to sin that we have, the old Adamic nature that we got from our parents. Where did they get it? Their parents. Where did they get it? From Adam! Like it or not, inside we all have an enemy called the flesh—an old sin nature. You know it is there. It's present in all of us.

Ephesians 2:3 says we are "by nature children of wrath." David said in the Psalms, "The wicked are estranged from the womb; they go astray as soon as they are born, speaking lies" (58:3). Have you ever thought about it: you never have to teach a little baby to lie? You have to teach a little baby to tell the truth. You don't have to teach a child to be selfish. You have to teach a child not to be selfish. We all have in us an enemy inside the gates called the flesh.

The Devil Made Me Do It

Some like to say, "The devil made me do it." I've got news for you, friend. If the devil were to evaporate, you'd go on sinning. You can't blame everything on the devil. There's enough inside of us to cause us to sin—that old desire that the Bible calls "the flesh."

A little boy spit on his sister, hit her with a broomstick, and called her a bad name. The mother said to this recalcitrant child, "Johnny, why did you do that? You shouldn't have done it; that was so bad! Johnny, the devil made you do that." He said, "The devil made me call her a bad name and hit her with a broomstick, but spitting on her was my idea." I think we'd be surprised if we knew how much really is our idea and how much of it is just pure flesh.

The Infernal Foe — the Devil

The devil is the *infernal* foe, and he is the mastermind behind all of these other things. Ephesians 6:12 says, "We do not wrestle against flesh and blood, but against principalities, against powers, against the rulers of the darkness of this age, against spiritual hosts of wickedness in the heavenly places."

You have an enemy—Lucifer, the devil. He is your foe. He has a plan to sabotage your life. He wants to ruin your life and bring death to happiness and purity and youth and wholeness. The devil is real, and he has organized against us. Let me show you how.

The Unholy Trinity of Temptation

The Bible says, "No temptation has overtaken you except such as is common to man" (1 Cor. 10:13). Whatever the temptation, it comes from one of these three sources:

- The world—the *external* foe
- The flesh—the *internal* foe
- The devil—the *infernal* foe

Together they are an unholy trinity of temptation that constantly works against us. Think of your flesh as a pool of gasoline. Think of the world as a lighted match. Think of the devil as the one who strikes the match and throws it. Then you just see how temptation comes about.

The Seat of Temptation

Where are you tempted? You can only be tempted in one of three areas because that's all there is. Do you know what your nature is made of? Body, soul, and spirit. And if you're tempted, you're going to have to be tempted in body, soul, or spirit.

In 1 Thessalonians 5:23, the apostle Paul says, "May your whole spirit, soul, and body be preserved blameless at the coming of our Lord Jesus Christ." This verse speaks of the nature of human nature— spirit, soul, and body. Now what does that mean—spirit, soul, and body? God is a triune God—Father, Son, and Holy Spirit. We are in His image, and we have a tri-unity to our own nature, just a faint representation of the tri-unity of Almighty God.

The First Seat of Temptation—the Body

The first part of your nature that is tempted is the body. The body is the most obvious because you can see it. The body is just a space suit that we wear so that we can live on planet Earth. The Bible calls that body our earthly house. We live in a body. Your bodily appetites can be a seat of temptation.

The Second Seat of Temptation—the Soul

Inside your body is a soul. The Greek word for "soul" is *psuche*. When the word is Anglicized, we get *psychic, psychiatry,* and *psychology.* Your soul is the psychological part of you—your mind, your emotion, and your will. Your soul is what makes you the wonderful person you are. It's your sense of humor, your intellect, your taste, your idiosyncrasies. Another word for *soul* is *ego* or *self.* The soul or ego is another seat of temptation.

The Third Seat of Temptation—the Spirit

What about your spirit? For a long time as a young Christian, I used to think soul and spirit were basically the same thing, the invisible part of us. But the Bible distinguishes between soul and spirit. Remember 1 Thessalonians 5:23: "May your whole spirit, soul, and body be preserved blameless." Or Hebrews 4:12, "For the word of God is living and powerful, and sharper than any two-edged sword, piercing even to the division of soul and spirit." There's a difference.

What is the spirit? The spirit is much like the soul in that it is invisible. Spirit and soul are indivisible, but they are not identical. The spirit in man is what makes man different from all of the other creatures. None of the other creatures have a spirit. Only man has a spirit because we are made in the image of God, and God is spirit. "God is Spirit, and those who worship Him must worship in spirit and truth" (John 4:24). When we get saved, "The Spirit Himself bears witness with our spirit that we are children of God" (Rom. 8:16). The spirit is that part of your nature that can know God, fellowship with God, commune with God.

Understanding Body, Soul, and Spirit

- With my body I have *physical* life, and I know the world beneath me.
- With my soul I have *psychological* life, and I know the world around me and within me.

- With my spirit I have *spiritual* life, and I know the world above me.

Plants have a body, but they don't have a spirit or a soul. Animals have a body and a soul (conscious life), but they don't have a spirit. Animals can't commune with God, pray, conceive of eternity, be redeemed by the precious love of Jesus Christ. Only man has a spirit.

I am made to know three worlds: the physical world, the psychological world, and the spiritual world—the world beneath me, the world within and around me, and the world above me.

Healthy, Happy, and Holy

When my body is right, I'm healthy. When my soul is right, I'm happy. When my spirit is right, I'm holy. And that's the way God intended for man to be. That's the way Adam was when he came off the assembly line. He was healthy in his body, happy in his soul, holy in his spirit; he was a whole person.

Most of the people I know are unhealthy, unhappy, and unholy. They are out of whack because they're not what God created them to be. That's what sin has done to the human race. When the devil comes to tempt, how does he tempt? In the body, the soul, or the spirit. Those are the only places you can be tempted because that's all there is.

You say, "OK, that's interesting, but how is that going to help me to overcome temptation?" Pay attention because I'm going to show you how this is practical, not merely theoretical. C. C. Mitchell wisely points out that there is a three-pronged attack on the spiritual life. I am grateful for his insight.[1]

The World Attacks the Soul

Remember, you have three enemies—the world, the flesh, and the devil. You're going to find out that each of those enemies is going to attack you in a particular part of your nature. The world is going to attack you primarily in the area of the soul. What is the soul? The ego, the self, the mind, the emotion, and the will. A worldly Christian is just a person whose mind, emotion, and will have been squeezed into an ungodly mold.

In the Bible there was a great man whose name was Abraham. Abraham had a nephew named Lot, and they were living in the land of Canaan. There began to be a range war because both of them were very wealthy, and they had all kinds of flocks and cattle. Their cowboys were arguing, and their shepherds were feuding.

So Abraham said to his nephew, "Look, Lot, let's not have any strife; we're brothers. Let's just divide this land. Just choose, Lot, wherever you want to go. You go in one direction, I'll go in the other. The land's before you—just choose." The Bible says that Lot pitched his tent toward the well-watered plains of Sodom where the grass was tall, green, and succulent.

When Lot went down there to Sodom, he got into all kinds of trouble because Sodom was a wicked, vile, horrible city. But why did he go down to Sodom? He did not go down to Sodom because it was a vile city. He did not go down there because of the sexual perversion. He went down there for one reason: there was good pasture down there. He wanted his flocks and his herds down there.

Why did he want that? He didn't need any more wealth. When man gets a certain amount of wealth, he doesn't need any more. Even Bill Gates can eat only one meal at a time, wear one suit of clothes at a time, sleep on one bed at a time. When men get to that point, they are not making money; they're keeping score. It is more of an ego trip than anything else.

What Lot wanted to do was to be the biggest rancher in all of Canaan. He wanted to be king of the hill. The world was attacking his ego, the soul. He was like many modern Americans. We may have "In God We Trust" on our money, but we have "Me First" on our hearts.

The Flesh Attacks the Body

What about the flesh? Where does the flesh tempt us? The flesh, our sinful nature, tempts us primarily in the area of the body. The body is not evil, but the old flesh will tempt us in the area of the body and our physical life. We're talking about sins of gluttony, violence, laziness, impurity, perversion. The flesh takes our physical body and makes it a vehicle for the expression of sensual sin.

An illustration of that is King David. King David committed the sin of adultery with Bathsheba. What happened? His flesh used his body as a vehicle for his sin, and he lusted after Bathsheba. He took Bathsheba, and then he committed a terribly egregious sin with her.

But was this a worldly temptation? Was he trying to be a big shot? Did he want everybody to know? No, he tried to hide it. He wasn't on an ego trip, not at all. But his body was under attack from his fleshly appetite.

When God says, "Flee fornication," when God says, "You shall not commit adultery," God is not trying to keep us from sex; God is trying to keep sex for us. It is a great, wonderful gift of God, but the devil is a pervert and will pervert that which is good and righteous and holy. So the devil takes the flesh, that old sin nature, and takes something like the body, which is good; and he twists it and perverts it. While the world wars against the soul, the flesh will war against the body.

The Devil Attacks the Spirit

What about the infernal foe, the devil? Where does he war? Where does he come against you? This may surprise you, but he comes not in the area of the body primarily but in the area of the spirit. The devil wars against your spirit. Remember, your spirit is the part of your nature that enables you to know and worship God, and that is the one thing the devil does not want. The devil wants to drive a wedge between you and God.

The devil doesn't necessarily want to make you a drunk. Perhaps he'd rather have you be a man of distinction at the country club. What kind of advertisement for the devil is an old drunk in the gutter in his own vomit covered with flies? He'd much rather have you a self-confident man, a man who thinks he can handle it all, that has no dependency upon God whatsoever. The devil is not against religion and manners. He'd just as soon send you to hell from the pew as from the gutter.

Jesus was on His way to Calvary, and He told His disciples that He was going to be crucified. Simon Peter said, "Lord, this will never happen to You. No, Lord!" And then later on he said, "Lord, if it happens, I'll go with You to prison and to death." And Jesus said, "Peter, before the rooster crows, you will three times deny that you know Me." Then He said, "Peter, Satan has desired you, that he may sift you as wheat, but I have prayed for you that your faith should not fail" (Luke 22:31–32, paraphrased).

Where was Satan working on Simon Peter? On his faith, his relationship with God. That's what the temptation was—to deny Jesus.

Peter wasn't on an ego trip. I'll guarantee you that. It wasn't his soul that was under attack. It wasn't that his hormones were raging, that he was going to commit some sexual sin or get drunk. No, his spirit was under attack—his faith got weak, and it was the old devil that was doing that.

Satan will come against you and me just like he attacked Simon Peter. When he does, the Bible tells us to use the "shield of faith" to protect against Satan's fiery darts of doubt (Eph. 6:16).

So the seats of temptation are the body, soul, and spirit. The world attacks primarily the soul; the flesh attacks primarily the body, and the devil attacks primarily the spirit.

The Seasons of Temptation

Now let's consider the seasons of temptation. You're going to find out that these temptations come through life in waves.

The Temptations of Youth

For example, when you're young, where is temptation? Primarily in the realm of the body, the sins of the body: sex, drugs, violence, laziness. These are, for the most part, the sins of youth.

The Temptations of Middle Age

The temptations of middle age come mainly from the world. By the way, I always laugh about middle age. You ask a man who is fifty-five, "How old are you?" He says, "I'm middle age." How many 110-year-old men do you know?

One of the primary sins of men and women of middle age is soulish sin. By then they've pretty much handled the sins of the flesh, but now they're into the sins of the soul, the ego, wanting to be the biggest—my lawn, my house, my car, my business, my achievements, my medals, my awards, my trophies, my this, my that. They spend their time chasing after the world, trying to be Mr. Big and Mrs. Big.

The Temptations of Old Age

You know what happens when we get real old. We've figured out that we're too old to run around like the kids, and we didn't really make it in middle age to be the big shot we wanted, but the devil still moves in on us. Do you know what the devil does to older people? He causes doubt and fear.

The devil comes in and says, "You know, you're going to get some nameless disease, you're going to die, your children won't be around to help you. Your retirement money is going to run out. God doesn't really love you. You're going to have problems." And the devil, that dirty devil, attacks in the realm of the spirit to bring fear and doubt.

Any temptation may come at any stage, but there do seem to be temptations that are stronger at certain ages.

The Subduing of Temptation

Think about subduing temptation. This is the good part. How do you get victory in the area of temptation? This is so wonderful. When you understand how the devil is working and how the flesh is working and how the world is working, then you understand how to get victory over these three areas. Let me give you *three key words*.

Against the World, the Key Word Is *Faith*

Against the external foe, the world, the key word is *faith*. "For whatsoever is born of God overcomes the world. And this is the victory that has overcome the world—our faith" (1 John 5:4). It is faith that overcomes the world. John continues in verse 5, "Who is he who overcomes the world, but he who believes that Jesus is the Son of God." It's not just faith in the general sense; it is specific faith in Jesus. Seeing that Jesus is the Son of God, *that* is the victory that overcomes the world.

How does that work? Remember what a worldly Christian is: that's somebody on an ego trip, somebody who is trying to satisfy life's hidden hunger with an ungodly system of values. What is a Christian? A Christian is somebody who has seen Jesus with the eye of faith, who realizes how wonderful Jesus is and has found his or her satisfaction in the Lord Jesus Christ. The Bible says in 1 John 2:15: "If anyone loves the world, the love of the Father is not in him." That's a tremendous verse. Now notice, it doesn't say you don't love the Father because you love the world. It is just the opposite— you love the world because the love of the Father is not in you.

What to Do When the Red Light Comes On

You're driving down the road in your automobile, and you look up on your dashboard. A red light comes on that you've never noticed before. It has the symbol of a little oil can on it. If you know anything about automobile mechanics, that light is a warning; it means you've lost the oil in the crankcase, and you're low on oil. If you continue to drive that way, you'll burn up the engine.

If that ever happens to you, and you see that little red light come on the dashboard, let me tell you what to do. Keep a hammer under your front seat. When that little light comes on, take the hammer and break it. It will go out and there'll be no more problems. That will take care of it—just take a hammer and break it.

Is that good advice? Of course not! That red light on the dashboard is only a warning. What is the warning? There's no oil in the crankcase, and attacking the light is not the answer.

You're never told to fight the world. If you're worldly, there's one reason you're worldly. You've got no spiritual oil in your crankcase. "If anyone loves the world, the love of the Father is not in him" (1 John 2:15). "This is the victory that has overcome the world—our faith" (1 John 5:4). It is faith that makes Jesus a reality in our lives. People who are worldly have never found their satisfaction in Jesus.

Everybody wants to be satisfied. The reason most people don't find satisfaction is that they are looking for it in the wrong place. When we see what we have in the Lord Jesus Christ, really understand who He is, this world has no allure for us because we are already satisfied.

If You're Satisfied with Steak, You Won't Want the Devil's Crumbs

What if you were to offer me a wonderful meal—a sizzling sirloin steak, a baked potato, a tossed salad, and a big, tall glass of iced tea. And how about some key lime pie for dessert? That would be great! And then after I eat that, suppose I go outside and somebody hands me a plate of stale crumbs or something that's rotten, and says, "Here, here's something to eat." I'd say, "No thank you, I'm already satisfied." When you're fed on Jesus, you don't have to be in the back alley eating tin cans with the devil's billy goats.

105

"If anyone loves the world, the love of the Father is not in him" (1 John 2:15). How do you deal with the sin of worldliness? Faith! We need to ask ourselves, "Do I really have faith?" This is the victory that overcomes the world—our faith. "Who is he who overcomes the world, but he who believes that Jesus is the Son of God" (1 John 5:5). "Turn your eyes upon Jesus, look full in his wonderful face, and the things of earth will grow strangely dim in the light of his glory and grace."[2] A worldly Christian is a person who has not found his or her satisfaction in Jesus Christ.

Against the Flesh, the Key Word Is *Flight*

When battling against the internal foe, the flesh, the key word is *flight*. "Flee also youthful lusts" (2 Tim. 2:22). "Flee sexual immorality" (1 Cor. 6:18). This is not a sin you are told to overcome by fighting; you're told to run. You're to flee! You're to be a first-class coward. First Corinthians 10:13 tells us, "God is faithful, who will not allow you to be tempted beyond what you are able, but with the temptation will make the way of escape." Sometimes that way of escape is the King's highway, two legs and a hard run. Just get out of there.

Jesus taught us to pray every morning, "Do not lead us into temptation" (Matt. 6:13). Don't watch that garbage on TV. Don't read those magazines. Why put that in your mind? You are flirting with temptation. You say, "I can read those dirty magazines; it doesn't bother me." If you're a man, and you read that and say it doesn't bother you, you're either no man, superman, or a liar. No, you can't put a fire in your bosom and not be burned. You should just flee from these things.

Time to Get the Twinkies Out

If you're wanting to lose weight, get those Twinkies out of the house. If you're trying to stop smoking cigarettes, don't put that carton in the dresser in case you go back—you *will!* Just get rid of it.

I thank God that I married a virgin. I went to the marriage altar a virgin. I had temptations. Every boy does. They told me as a kid, "A boy becomes what he thinks about." It's a wonder I didn't turn into a girl! In college I kept a motto on my desk: "He who would not fall down ought not to walk in slippery places." "Flee fornication." "Flee youthful lusts." Don't see how close you can get to it; don't dabble. That's like playing with fire, like playing with matches and dry grass.

Parents, when your kids go out on a date, they don't need to go to some secluded rendezvous. Let them go to the football game with fifty thousand people around. Then when they come home, if they know each other well enough and it's time for a goodnight kiss, let them do it on the front step under the porch light with dad looking through the keyhole with a shotgun.

Bottom line—don't put yourself into those kinds of temptations.

Joseph and Mrs. Potiphar

Joseph in the Bible was under fleshly attack from a woman named Mrs. Potiphar. (We don't know what her first name was, except that she was the wife of Potiphar.) Joseph was the housekeeper, the manager, and Potiphar was the head of the KGB, the Egyptian army. Mrs. Potiphar looked at young Joseph. He was evidently a handsome dude. She wanted to have an affair with him. One day she took him by his garment and tried to pull him into bed. Joseph was petrified. He came out of his coat and left it in her hand. He saturated that place with his absence. He just got out of there.

I know some preachers today that are so stupid. I think they would have said, "Now Mrs. Potiphar, you ought not to act that way. Let's you and I kneel down by the bed and pray about this thing." Don't ever try to do something that dumb. You can't reason with or resist the sins of the flesh. God's answer is to run as fast as you can in the opposite direction!

Against the Devil, the Key Word Is *Fight*

When we come to the devil, we are in a battle. The Bible says in Ephesians 6:12: "For we do not wrestle against flesh and blood, but against principalities, against powers, . . . against spiritual hosts of wickedness in the heavenly places." The Bible says in the book of James, "Resist the devil and he will flee from you" (4:7).

Never run from the devil—never. You can't outrun him. When you get where you're going, he'll already be there ahead of you. You turn around, and you resist the devil in the name of Jesus. Against the world faith, against the flesh flight, but against the devil fight.

People say, "I'm not afraid of the devil." That's not the big question. Is the devil afraid of you? He ought to be. You can come against Satan in the name of Jesus, and according to James 4:7, "He will flee from you." In Revelation 12:11, the Bible says, "And they overcame him [the devil] by the blood of the Lamb and by the word of their testimony, and they did not love their lives to the death." You can actually overcome the devil.

Tell the Devil to Take a Hike

The next time the devil gets on your trail, and you understand that the devil is trying to drive a wedge between you and God, you don't have to take it. You can resist him. First, make sure there's no sin in your life, sin that is unconfessed and unrepented. Get your heart clean. Then if the devil gets on your trail, you can say to him, "Devil, I resist you, and I rebuke you, and I come against you in the name of Jesus Christ. I am saved. My sin is under the blood. I have been twice born. My body is the temple of the Holy Spirit of God. Your back was broken at Calvary. You have no right, you have no authority in my life. You're a pervert. You're trespassing on my Father's property and in the name of Jesus, be gone!" He'll flee from you. You say, "Isn't that like praying to the devil?" I'm not praying to a cat when I say, "Scat!"

You Can Know Victory

Friend, God has given us the victory. "No temptation has overtaken you except such as is common to man; but God is faithful, who will not allow you to be tempted beyond what you are able" (1 Cor. 10:13).

- Against the world—*faith*. Fall in love with Jesus!
- Against the flesh—*flight*. Get out of there!
- Against the devil—*fight*. You resist him because greater is He that is in you than he that is in the world.

Let's live victoriously. May the Father seal this truth to your heart! You *can* know victory and turn temptation into triumph.

6

Every Christian Ought to Know

ABOUT BELIEVERS BAPTISM

Go therefore and make disciples of all the nations, baptizing them in the name of the Father and of the Son and of the Holy Spirit, teaching them to observe all things that I have commanded you.

MATTHEW 28:19–20

Baptism is one of the most important, meaningful, and beautiful experiences in the Christian life. You will be greatly blessed when you submit to it. I am not speaking about church tradition but Bible baptism. You might sometimes hear someone refer to "that Baptist doctrine of baptism by immersion." It's not a Baptist doctrine. If Baptists have Baptist doctrine, they need to get rid of it. We also need to do away with Methodist doctrine, Episcopalian doctrine, and Roman Catholic doctrine, as such, and go to what the Bible says.

If what I show you is not in the Bible, then don't believe it. If it is in the Bible, say, "That is God's Word, and that's what I'm going to stand on."

Someone may say, "Baptism—that's just incidental. It really doesn't make any difference." I want to destroy that philosophy, if that is your philosophy. Baptism is not incidental; it is fundamental. Don't ever minimize what God has so maximized.

Think of the ministry of the Lord Jesus Christ. He had a ministry of three and a half years. How did He commence His ministry? By being baptized. How did He conclude His ministry? By commanding baptism—the Great Commission. He said, "All authority has been given to Me. . . . Go therefore and make disciples of all the nations, baptizing them in the name of the Father and of the Son and of the Holy Spirit, teaching them to observe all things that I have commanded you" (Matt. 28:18–20).

Jesus commanded it. We are not to minimize something that Jesus taught about so strongly and emphasized so much. I'm going to show you why baptism is such an important doctrine in the Word of God.

The Method of Baptism—Immersion

Some say, "The Bible teaches all kinds of baptism—sprinkling, immersion, pouring." No, it doesn't. There is only one kind of water baptism taught in the Bible, and that is immersion.

Example of Jesus

Let's see how Jesus Christ was baptized. In Mark 1:9 (KJV), we see a picture of the baptism of Jesus: "And it came to pass in those days, that Jesus came from Nazareth of Galilee, and was baptized of John in Jordan." The Jordan referred to here is the River Jordan. Jesus was not baptized near or with Jordan; He was baptized *in* Jordan. Verse 10 continues: "And straightway coming up out of the water." Now, if He came up out of the water, where was He? Down in the water! Black print on white paper makes it obvious that Jesus was baptized by immersion.

By the way, why did Jesus take this trip? The Bible says He came from Nazareth of Galilee to where John was in Jordan. That's about sixty miles. This was not a baptism of convenience. John wasn't baptizing down there because of the scenery. I've been down there, and it's not a pretty place. Why was John the Baptist down there baptizing? We don't have to guess. We know why he was there because the Bible tells us why in John 3:23: "And John also was baptizing in Aenon near to Salim, because there was *much water there* (KJV)." If we baptize by sprinkling, we could baptize seven thousand people with a jugful. The reason John was baptizing down there is simple: there was much water there, and it takes a lot of water to baptize.

It's Not Convenient to Baptize

Sometimes it's inconvenient to baptize. I was in Kenya, out from Nairobi, and I went out on a mission trip with several others to visit the tribe of tall native warriors called the Masai. We went out there in the backlands in a Land Rover and saw the gazelles jumping, along with ostriches, zebras, and ant hills over six feet high. As we went farther and farther out there, with Kilimanjaro in view, we came to a little Masai village where our missionary friend had been preaching the gospel of Jesus Christ.

When these Masai got saved, they wanted to be baptized. There was no pond out there, so they dug a pit, which looked exactly like a grave to me, and lined it with plastic. Then they brought water with the Land Rover and poured it in there. And those people were being baptized in a gravelike hole. This is fitting because baptism really pictures a burial. Now, why all of that difficulty? Wouldn't it have been a lot easier just to take out a canteen and sprinkle everybody?

The Fire Department to the Rescue

Baptism is difficult sometimes. In the first church I pastored after I got out of school, the baptistery had a small pipe for water with a diameter about the size of my thumb. Consequently, it took a long time to fill that baptistery with enough water to baptize people.

I had announced that we were going to have baptismal services on Sunday afternoon, and we had some people coming from out of town. When I got to the church, I looked in the baptistery. It was bone dry. The janitor had forgotten to turn on the water, and I knew that it would take all afternoon to get that baptistery filled.

I said, "Dear God, what am I going to do?" I had a moment of inspiration; I called the fire department. I said, "Do you specialize in emergencies?" They said, "Yes," and I said, "Well, I've got one." I talked them into sending a pumper truck over. They filled that baptistery up lickety-split with rusty water, but I got the people baptized. It would have been much easier to do it some other way, but it takes immersion to baptize.

The first person I ever baptized as a young pastor, I baptized in a creek down in Florida. I led Willie Vereen to Christ, and she wanted to be baptized. I didn't know how to baptize. I hardly knew where to take hold of the person, but we went slithering down that muddy bank into that creek water outside. What a joy that was. It was a cold day for Florida, and when her feet hit that cold water, she went "Sheeeeeee," but then we went into that water, and I baptized her.

It's not convenient to baptize this way. Remember that Jesus went from Nazareth of Galilee down to the muddy old Jordan to be baptized. Why? "John . . . was baptizing in Aenon near to Salim because there was much water there" (John 3:23). Too many people are looking for convenience rather than standing on conviction. Soon I'm expecting some churches to take members in over the telephone and baptize their photographs. Seriously, we should not be looking for a convenient faith.

Example of Philip and the Ethiopian

In Acts 8, there's the story of Philip. He'd been led out in the desert by the Spirit. He met an Ethiopian who was traveling. He had been to Jerusalem to worship, and Philip met him out there and led him to Christ. The man then wanted to be baptized. We pick up the story in Acts 8:36: "Now as they went down the road, they came to some water. And the eunuch said, 'See, here is water. What hinders me from being baptized?'" This man, this eunuch, was the treasurer for Queen Candace of Ethiopia. He was traveling by chariot. You know they had drinking water. You know they had bathing water. It wasn't that they needed a little cup of water for a sprinkling service.

Continuing in verses 37–38, "Philip said, 'If you believe with all your heart you may.' And he answered and said, 'I believe that Jesus Christ is the Son of God.' So he commanded the chariot to stand still." Now notice this: "And both Philip and the eunuch went down into the water, and he baptized him." Now let's translate: "And they went both down into the water, both Philip and the eunuch and he *immersed* him." Verse 39 continues: "Now when they came up out of the water [If they came up out of the water, where were they? In the water.], the Spirit of the Lord caught Philip away, so that the eunuch saw him no more; and he went on his way rejoicing." The point is made one more time: Bible baptism is by immersion. It is not always convenient, but that is the method of baptism.

Example of the Early Church

Baptism by immersion was originally practiced by all branches and sects of the early Christian church. Baptism by sprinkling or pouring initially began being used as a way to baptize the sick or bedridden, but baptism by immersion was the preferred method. Baptism by sprinkling was adopted only by the Roman Catholic Church as the predominant method in the thirteenth century.

This is evident in the writings of the early church fathers:

Tertullian, AD 200: "We are immersed."

Cyril, Bishop of Jerusalem, AD 348: "The body is dipped in water."

Vitringa: "The act of baptizing is the immersion of believers in water. Thus, also, it was performed by Christ and his apostles."

The late first-century/early second-century Epistle of Barnabas contains the following description of Christian baptism: "We indeed descend into the water full of sins and defilement, but come up, bearing fruit in our heart, having the fear [of God] and trust in Jesus in our spirit."

"This baptism, therefore, is given into the death of Jesus: the water is instead of the burial . . . the *descent into the water* the dying together with Christ; the *ascent out of the water* the rising again with him."[1]

Hippolytus preserves an early baptismal creed in his writings: "When the person being baptized *goes down into the water,* he who baptizes him, putting his hand on him, shall say: 'Do you believe in God, the Father Almighty?' And the person being baptized shall say: 'I believe.'"[2]

It may also surprise you to find that many of the founders and leaders of denominations that practice sprinkling have in their writings acknowledged immersion as the original biblical method.

George Whitefield (Methodist), commenting on Romans 6:4: "It is certain that the words of our text is an allusion to the manner of baptism by *immersion.*"

Conybeare and Howson (Episcopalians) commenting on Romans 6:4: "This passage cannot be understood unless it is understood that the primitive baptism was by *immersion.*"

John Calvin (Presbyterian): "The very word *baptize,* however, signifies to immersion, and it is certain that immersion was the practice of the ancient church."[3]

Martin Luther (Lutheran): "I could wish that the baptized should be totally *immersed* according to the meaning of the word."

Philip Schaff (Lutheran): "Immersion and not sprinkling was unquestionably the original normal form of baptism. This is shown by the meaning of the Greek word and the analogy of the baptism of John which was performed in Jordan."[4]

As a matter of fact, if you travel to Europe sometime, go into some of the old cathedrals. I'm talking about Roman Catholic cathedrals built before the thirteenth century, and you'll find some have baptisteries in them like we have in churches that immerse, pools where one can be immersed.

Baptism in the Christian church began with the practice of total immersion which followed the example set by Jesus. Until Christianity was made legal, early Christians baptized converts in streams or in private homes. However, after the fourth century legalization of Christianity, congregations began to build separate buildings expressly for baptism. This continued until the practice of total immersion faded from popular use in the Middle Ages. Examples of early total immersion type baptisteries are plentiful. The one beside The Leaning Tower of Pisa is simply one among many. Historians say there are sixty-seven (total immersion type) baptisteries still in existence in Italy today that date from the fourth to the fourteenth century.

Baptisteries, such as the one at Pisa, were built separate from the church because baptisms were usually conducted only three or four times a year (Christmas, Easter, Pentecost, Epiphany). In some cases, hundreds of people were baptized by the bishop, given white robes and then invited to join the rest of the church family in the cathedral next door. However, over the years, it seems that it became easier to simply pour a little water over the candidate or even sprinkle a few drops (called affusion) upon them. A Roman Catholic, Cardinal Gibbons, stated, "For several centuries after the establishment of Christianity, baptism was usually conferred by immersion, but since the twelfth century the practice of baptizing by affusion has prevailed in the Catholic Church, as this manner is attended with less inconvenience than baptism by immersion."[5]

Baptize—an Untranslated Word

Did you know that the word *baptize* is basically an untranslated word in your Bible? It's really a Greek word, meaning "to immerse." King James of England commissioned the scholars in 1611 to translate the Scriptures into English. For the New Testament they went back to the original Greek manuscripts. When they came to this word *baptize,* which literally means "to immerse," it created a problem. The word was used in ordinary language, not as a religious word. A woman doing dishes would baptize her dishes, or immerse them. If two little boys were out playing in the water, instead of saying, "I'm going to dunk you," one of them would say, "I'm going to baptize you."

It had nothing to do with religion as such.[6] The word simply means "to immerse." It's just a plain, ordinary word, not necessarily a religious word. It now has religious significance.

The word *baptize* is an untranslated word. It has been transliterated—taken from one language and put into another language. Why didn't they translate it? The king at that time and his church practiced sprinkling, and he was the one who said, "Translate the Scriptures."

These scholars had a problem. If they took that word and translated it as *sprinkling,* anybody who knew Greek would have laughed them out of the kingdom. But on the other hand, if they translated it as *immerse,* then it would be a source of embarrassment to the king. So what you read in your Bible is an untranslated word. They just took the word *baptizo,* made a new English word out of it, and placed it into the English language.

So each time, if you want to, when you're reading the word *baptize,* you can just do your own translation in your mind. The word means "to immerse." In the Greek language *epicheō* means "to pour," *rhantizō* means "to sprinkle," *baptizō* means "to immerse." Scripture doesn't use those other words for baptism; it only uses the word *baptizo,* which means "to put under the water or immerse."

Sometimes people say, "Ah, but sprinkling is taught in the Bible," and they'll find somewhere, some ceremony where there is the sprinkling of water, or a sacrifice and the sprinkling of blood. Granted, the word *sprinkling* is used, but it has nothing to do with baptism. I defy anybody to show me anywhere in the Bible where sprinkling is taught as a form of baptism. It just simply is not there.

The Meaning of Baptism

The meaning and the method are inextricably interwoven. If you change the method, you will destroy the meaning. The method and the meaning are bound together.

Baptism Pictures the Saving Work of Jesus Christ

In Romans 6:4–7 Paul says, "Therefore we were buried with Him [that is, with Jesus] through baptism into death, that just as Christ was raised from the dead by the glory of the Father, even so we also should walk in newness of life. For if we have been united together in the likeness of His death, certainly we also shall be in the likeness of His resurrection, knowing this, that our old man was crucified with Him, that the body of sin might be done away with, that we should no longer be slaves of sin. For he who has died has been freed from sin."

This passage says that baptism is the picture of the death, burial, and resurrection of Jesus Christ and our death, burial, and resurrection with Him. Remember this: baptism pictures and symbolizes the saving gospel of Jesus Christ. That's the reason we say we must adhere to the method because if you change the method, you destroy the picture.

Waterfall or Coffee Table—Any Picture Will Do

Suppose you've never seen my wife Joyce, and you say, "Adrian, are you married?"

"Yes."

"What's your wife like? Do you have a picture of her?"

I'd say, "Yes I do. Would you like to see a picture of her?"

"Yes."

So I reach in my billfold, and I pull out a picture. Maybe I show you a picture of a racing car or a waterfall or a coffee table. And you say, "That's your wife?"

"No," I reply, "but any picture will do."

Wouldn't that be ridiculous? If it doesn't look like her, why should I give you a picture of a waterfall or a coffee table and say, "There's my wife"? It doesn't follow; it doesn't picture.

Baptism is a *picture* of a death and a burial and a resurrection. You can't picture a burial by sprinkling a few drops of water on anybody's head. When you go under the water, you are placed in a liquid tomb. "We [are] buried with him through baptism." When we come out of the water, that pictures a resurrection. We are raised to walk in newness of life (see Rom. 6:4).

What is the gospel? "Christ died for our sins according to the Scriptures, and that He was buried, and that He rose again the third day" (1 Cor. 15:3–4). That's the gospel. And *that's* what baptism pictures—our identification with the Lord Jesus and His saving gospel.

When Jesus was baptized, He was picturing His death, burial, and resurrection for us. When we're baptized, we're picturing our identification *with* His death, burial, and resurrection for us.

Death and Burial

Romans 6:4 says that "we were buried with Him through baptism into death." The baptistery is a liquid tomb, and it's a funeral service.

When I got baptized, it was just a funeral for the old Adrian. The old Adrian died, and baptism pictured the burial of the old Adrian. The only mourner there was the devil. He hated to see me die. I was his good buddy. And so the old Adrian is dead and buried.

Here's the reason one should never be baptized before he or she is truly saved. If you're baptized before you're truly saved, that would be like having your funeral before you die. When you're saved, you die to the old way; you say, "Good-bye old world, good-bye," and you become a new person. Baptism pictures that!

"Then those who gladly received his word were baptized; and that day about three thousand souls were added to them" (Acts 2:41). First they received the word, and then they were baptized. Acts 10:46–47: "For they heard them speak with tongues and magnify God. Then Peter answered, 'Can anyone forbid water, that these should not be baptized who have received the Holy Spirit just as we have?'" First, you receive the Holy Spirit, and then you're baptized.

In Acts 16:31–33, Paul and Silas said to the Philippian jailer, "Believe on the Lord Jesus Christ, and you will be saved, you and your household. Then they spoke the word of the Lord to him and to all who were in his house. And he took them the same hour of the night and washed their stripes. And immediately he and all his family were baptized." *First,* he heard the word of the Lord, he believed on Jesus, and *then* he was baptized.

New Life

When you're baptized, you're picturing your death with Jesus. But baptism not only pictures the burial of Jesus and your burial with Him, but it also pictures the resurrection of Jesus and your resurrection with Him. Not only are you buried by baptism, but also according to the Scripture, you are raised again.

Romans 6:4 says that we're raised to "walk in newness of life." You see, it's more than submersion; it's *immersion.* What's the difference? With submersion you may not come back up. You'll like the difference! You go down, you're put under the water, and then you come up out of the water raised to walk in newness of life. We say good-bye to the old world; we say hello to the new man.

Just Think of It!

Just think of what this pictures. I have been delivered from my sin! My sin is buried in the grave of God's forgetfulness, hallelujah! I am a new person. Baptism not only pictures my death with Him, my resurrection life with Him, but it pictures my ultimate glorification with Him. Romans 6:5 says, "We also shall be in the likeness of His resurrection."

One of these days I am going to have a body like the resurrection body of the Lord Jesus Christ. All of that is pictured in baptism—the death, burial, and resurrection of Jesus for our sin—and our identification with His death, burial, and resurrection.

If you were the devil and you could take any message out of the church, but only one, which one would you want to take out? The gospel! You wouldn't have to think about it. The devil doesn't care what you believe as long as you don't believe the gospel. What is the one ordinance that teaches the gospel over and over and over again? It's baptism. "Therefore we were buried with Him through baptism into death, that just as Christ was raised from the dead by the glory of the Father, even so we also should walk in newness of life. For if we have been united together in the likeness of His death, certainly we also shall be in the likeness of His resurrection" (Rom. 6:4–5). The devil's done a slick job on some people to take this wonderful picture of the gospel out of many of our churches.

Suppose I were to die, and you haul me out to the graveyard and say, "Let's bury Adrian." If you put a few grains of sand on my head and leave me to bake in the sun, that would be a disgrace. You can't bury me with a few grains of sand; you can't bury me with a few drops of water. We are buried with Him by baptism into death. What does baptism symbolize? It pictures the death, burial, and resurrection of Jesus.

Great Doctrines Are Taught by Baptism

Baptism pictures Calvary, it pictures Easter, it pictures Pentecost, it pictures the Second Coming because just as I come up out of that water, at the second coming of Jesus, though my body may be in the grave, I'm coming up out of that grave, just like I came up out of that water. These are magnificent truths that are taught by illustration in baptism.

The Motive for Baptism

So far in this chapter we've studied the biblical method of baptism, and I hope that I have shown you that the method is immersion. It is clear from the way people were baptized in the Bible that they were baptized by immersion. I've shown you the meaning. Baptism pictures the saving work of Jesus Christ. Now let's move to the third and final point—the motive for baptism. Let me give you a threefold motive.

A Master to Confess

You are identified with the Lord Jesus when you are baptized. Baptism shows that you are a new man or woman and that you have a new master. It shows that you are not ashamed of Christ. When you are baptized in front of all those people, you are saying, "I believe in Jesus."

In the Bible the confession of faith was not walking down the church aisle. Many times they didn't have church buildings, as such. The confession of faith was baptism. When one got baptized, he said, "I believe in Jesus Christ. I identify myself with His death, burial, and resurrection. I am not ashamed of Jesus."

Getting Baptized Doesn't Make *You Saved;* *It* Shows *You Are Saved*

Don't ever think that baptism saves you or even helps to save you; that would be a tragic mistake. But baptism pictures your salvation; it is a beautiful illustration of what happened when you got saved.

It's like the wedding ring I wear. That ring does not make me married. I could be married and not wear it. Some people might wear a ring but not be married. Wearing it doesn't make me married, and taking it off doesn't keep me from being married. But do you know what that ring means? It means I'm not ashamed of Joyce; I'm not trying to fool anybody. I am a married man, and I belong to that sweet girl. The ring is just a symbol, an emblem that I belong to her, and I'm not ashamed of it.

Baptism is just your way of saying, "I belong to Jesus Christ. I have been buried with Him, His death has my name on it, and I have been raised with Him. His resurrection is the resurrection life that I am living, and I belong to Him."

Once you have been saved, whenever possible, and as soon as possible, you should be baptized. But never, ever mistake the symbolism.

You Need to Get "Advertised"

One Sunday morning in children's church, a little boy prayed to receive Jesus into his heart. The children's pastor said, "Go tell the pastor that you've been saved, and you need to be baptized." The little boy went to the pastor and said, "Look, I have been saved; I need to get advertised." I like that! That's what it is: when you get baptized, you're getting advertised. You're saying, "Hey, look! I belong to Jesus Christ."

A Message to Convey

I have seen it so many times that when a person gets baptized, his friends and loved ones fall under conviction. It is preaching the gospel of Jesus Christ without saying a word. It's a silent but graphic sermon. It's saying, "Look, by my baptism, I am picturing the death, burial, and resurrection of Jesus Christ. The old person I used to be is dead. I am giving myself to the One who has died for me; I am no longer my own."

The Scripture says that I am raised to "walk in newness of life" (Rom. 6:4). Who would not want to preach that sermon before his loved ones? Who would not want to give that testimony if they're truly saved? I am convinced some women don't want to get baptized because they don't want to mess up their twenty-five dollar hairdo, some trivial thing, or they just don't want to go through that ordeal, when Jesus hung naked on the cross for them and died in agony and blood. No, there's a Master to confess, there's a message to convey, and third, there is a mandate to complete.

A Mandate to Complete

Jesus did not request you to be baptized, He commanded you to be baptized. The Great Commission, in Matthew 28:19 says, "Go therefore and make disciples of all the nations, baptizing them in the name of the Father and of the Son and of the Holy Spirit."

Now suppose I were to have a coronary and fall down on the ground and try to say something. You would say, "He's dying; he's trying to say something. Listen to him. These are his last words. He must think this is important."

Friend, when Jesus was concluding His ministry, He had some last words before He went back to heaven: "Baptizing them in the name of the Father and of the Son and of the Holy Spirit, teaching them to observe all things that I have commanded you; and lo, I am with you always, even to the end of the age" (Matt. 28:19–20). Don't minimize what our Lord has maximized. In Acts 10:48, when Cornelius and his household got saved, the Bible says Peter "commanded them to be baptized in the name of the Lord."

"If You Love Me, Keep My Commandments"—John 14:15

While baptism is not necessary to salvation, it is necessary to obedience, and obedience is necessary to joy and fruitfulness in the Christian life. Sometimes you might wonder, "Why can't I understand more of the Bible? Why don't I have more power in my life? O God, teach me what this verse means. Lord, I don't understand this verse; Lord, teach me that verse." God says, "I'm not going to teach you anything." "Why not, Lord?" "Well, I already showed you about baptism. You wouldn't get baptized, so why should I show you anything else? Why should I give you any more light when I have given you clear, plain light about this and you refuse it?"

The Bible says, "For whoever has, to him more will be given; but whoever does not have, even what he has will be taken away from him" (Mark 4:25). The way to understand the part of the Scripture you don't understand is to obey the part you do understand. When you begin to obey the part you do understand, you'll be surprised how much more new light will break into your life.

There is a Master to confess, there is a message to convey, there is a mandate to complete. God has commanded us to be baptized.

Again I want to make clear that baptism with a spoonful or a tank full cannot take away sin. You can be saved anytime, any place. If baptism is necessary to salvation, then a man in the desert can't be saved. A man in an airplane couldn't be saved. A man in a submarine surrounded by the ocean couldn't be saved because there's not enough water there to baptize him. No, anytime anybody anyplace calls upon Jesus in repentance and faith, they will be saved.

Don't Take the "Whosoever" out of the Bible

If you make baptism necessary, you have to take "whosoever" out of the Bible. You have to change it to say, "Whosoever believes in the Lord Jesus Christ *and* is fortunate enough to be near water *and* is fortunate enough to have a preacher around of my denomination shall be saved." No, the Bible says clearly, plainly, sweetly, sublimely, "Believe on the Lord Jesus Christ and you'll be saved."

This is a true story. In the sixties, when Lyndon Johnson was the president of the United States, a friend of mine and his children visited the Smithsonian Museum of American History in Washington, D.C. They came to the museum's First Ladies Collection, which features wax figures of each of the first ladies since 1909, wearing their actual inaugural gowns. They were especially interested in the wax figure of Lady Bird Johnson, who at that time was the current first lady.

As they stood there and were talking, they noticed someone standing beside them. They looked, and it was Lady Bird Johnson! She had come to see the dress. They were so thrilled; they thought, *This is the most wonderful thing; look here, she's right here with us.*

Just then, a man came with a camera and said, "Folks, would you mind just stepping aside a little bit. I want to get a picture of Lady Bird." He was just talking about the wax figure. Lady Bird was standing right there, and he said to her, "Would you move, please? Would you get out of the way? I want to get a picture of Lady Bird."

Think about it. It's not baptism that saves us; it's the death, burial, and resurrection of Jesus Christ that saves us. Don't ever substitute the emblem and the symbol for the reality.

Bible Baptism

Let's sum it up: Baptism, as taught in the Bible, has a *method,* a *meaning,* and a *motive.*

- The method—immersion. Remember, if you change the method, you destroy the meaning.
- The meaning—a picture of our identification with the death, burial, and resurrection of Jesus, which is the gospel.
- The motive for baptism is to confess Christ, obey Him, and declare His saving gospel.

If you are saved and not yet baptized, make plans as soon as possible to present yourself for this wonderful experience.

7

Every Christian Ought to Know

HOW TO DISCERN THE
WILL OF GOD

---

*"In all your ways acknowledge Him, and He shall
direct your paths."*

PROVERBS 3:6

Let's think about the will of God for your life. Your great *desire*
ought to be to know His will. Your great *delight* will be to do His
will. Your great *danger* is to refuse His will. Nothing is right for you
if it is not God's will.

131

Six Myths Concerning the Will of God

There are about six myths concerning the will of God, and I want to help destroy those myths in your mind.

1. The Map Myth

The first is what I call the *Map Myth,* that is, that God is going to give you a road map for His will for you. God does not give you a road map, and I'm glad He doesn't because if He did, it would be boring, and it would take all of the romance out of it. God doesn't do that. The will of God is not a road map; it is a relationship, so don't get the idea that God is going to say, "Now, five years from now you're going to be doing this; ten years from now you're going to be doing that. You're going to be over here for three years, and then you're going to be over there for two years." No, God does not do that. Do you remember how God led the children of Israel into the wilderness? A pillar of cloud by day; a pillar of fire by night. They didn't have to know where they were going. All they had to do was ask, "Can I see that pillar of cloud; can I see that pillar of fire?" And that's what you need to know: do I have His presence, His conscious presence, with me?

2. The Misery Myth

The second myth is the *Misery Myth*: if I do the will of God, it's going to be painful. God is some sort of a celestial killjoy. And Lord, if I say I will do anything You want me to do—anywhere, anytime, any place, any cost—I'll end up a missionary in deepest Africa; maybe I will be eaten by cannibals or something like that.

Some people are afraid of God. They really are afraid to surrender to the Lord. Yet God is a loving God, and God wants for us what we would want for ourselves if we had enough sense to want it. God is a loving God; don't believe the misery myth.

3. The Missionary Myth

And then there's what I call the *Missionary Myth*: God's will is just for a certain class of people. God calls preachers and God calls missionaries, but God doesn't call ordinary people. Listen, God has a plan for the evangelist, and He has a plan for the secretary. He has a plan for the preacher, and He has a plan for the plumber. He has a plan for the Bible teacher and the banker. God has a plan for all of us. So don't say, "I hope these missionaries can feel God's call; I hope these preachers can feel God's call in their life." Report for duty no matter who you are.

4. The Miracle Myth

Next is the *Miracle Myth*—that you must have something dramatic in order for you to know the will of God. You've got to see some sign or hear some voice or something like that.

While God may speak to you in a miracle, generally He does not. In 1 Kings 19:11–12, God was speaking to Elijah, and He said, "'Go out, and stand on the mountain before the LORD.' And behold, the LORD passed by, and a great and strong wind tore into the mountains and broke the rocks in pieces before the LORD, but the LORD was not in the wind; and after the wind an earthquake, but the LORD was not in the earthquake; and after the earthquake a fire, but the LORD was not in the fire; and after the fire a still small voice."

Many people I know want to be "Earthquakers" rather than "Quakers." They want a cyclone, they want a forest fire, they want an inferno, they want an earthquake so they will know the will of

God. If you want to find out generally the will of God for your life, there's a still, small voice and "the path of the just is like the shining sun, that shines ever brighter unto the perfect day" (Prov. 4:18). First it's dark, and then it's gray dawn, and then you see colors and shadows, and after a while it's high noon. And soon you're knowing the will of God for your life.

5. The Missed-It Myth

Then there's the *Missed-It Myth.* You say, "I missed it. When I was young, God had a plan for my life, and now that I'm old, I think maybe God wanted me to be a missionary, and so it's too late for me."

It's never too late for you. God has a will for your life and every stage of your life. You may have missed God's original plan for you, but I love this verse: In Joel 2:25, God says, "I will restore to you the years that the swarming locust has eaten." Isn't that great? So, if you've had some years that you think were wasted, let God give you a fresh start.

Flying by God's "Mission Control"

I was serving a church at Cape Kennedy when I first learned about guided missiles. Every missile on the launching pad has a plan, a trajectory, a carefully prescribed path for that missile to fly. Yet hardly a one of them ever flies according to that original plan. They have on-board computers, and those thrusters begin to yaw and gimbal, and if a missile strays from that first plan, then they replan it. If it goes astray again, they replan it—they keep on replanning. It perhaps never is following the originally prescribed plan, but it's never out from under control.

If you missed God's plan, just let God reprogram you where you are. However, if one of those missiles turned around and headed back toward the launching pad, they pushed the button and boom! That's it. Don't ever let that happen to you.

Don't rebel against God, but don't think that it's too late for you if you perhaps missed God's plan.

6. The Mystery Myth

Last of all, there's the *Mystery Myth*—that God's will is a mystery; it's sort of like an Easter egg hunt. God says, "There's something I want you to do, but I'm not going to tell you what it is. You search and see if you can find it." That's kind of absurd. It would be like me saying to my son, "Now son, there are some things I want you to do. If you do them, you'll be very happy, and I'll reward you. If you don't do them, I'm going to punish you, and you'll be very unhappy." He says, "Well, Dad, since you've explained it to me, what do you want me to do?" "I'm not going to tell you. You can figure it out, but you'd better not miss it." No, no, no. That would be ridiculous. God *wants* you to know His will.

Let's Clear Up These Myths

If you could meet Jesus face-to-face, in the flesh, and ask Him one question about you, what would you ask Him? I think I know what I would ask Him. It would be this: "Lord, what do You want me to do?"

The apostle Paul asked Him that question when he met Him on the road to Damascus in Acts 9. I don't know a better chapter in all of the Bible that tells us how to know the will of God for our lives than this chapter.

"Then Saul, [that was his name before he became the great apostle Paul] still breathing threats and murder against the disciples of the Lord, went to the high priest and asked letters from him to the synagogues of Damascus, so that if he found any who were of the Way, ["the Way" is the name they gave Christians—"people of the Way"] whether men or women, he might bring them bound to Jerusalem" (Acts 9:1–2). They were taking them prisoner and bringing them to Jerusalem. Some of them were put in prison; others were put to death.

"As he journeyed he came near Damascus, and suddenly a light shone around him from heaven. Then he fell to the ground, and heard a voice saying to him, 'Saul, Saul, why are you persecuting Me?' And he said, 'Who are You, Lord?' Then the Lord said, 'I am Jesus, whom you are persecuting. It is hard for you to kick against the goads.' So he, trembling and astonished, said, 'Lord, what do You want me to do?'" This question is the key that we're going to be discussing—how to know the will of God. "Then the Lord said to him, 'Arise and go into the city, and you will be told what you must do'" (Acts 9:3–6).

This is a wonderful promise to Saul about knowing the will of God for his life. We're going to find some principles as to how we can know the will of God for our lives. Saul asked two great questions in this passage of Scripture:

- First, "Who are You, Lord?"
- Next, "What do You want me to do?"

Can you think of two greater questions? "Lord, who are You?" and, "Lord, what do You want me to do?"

Paul spent the rest of his life learning the answer to those two great questions—just exactly who Jesus is, and what Jesus would have him to do. Today we need to ask the same questions.

Guided Missiles—Misguided Men and Women

Man has been described as a clever creature who has lost his way in the dark. This is an age when we're not surprised at anything that might happen. Technology is coming at us so fast it is like we are drinking from a fire hose.

However, in this age of guided missiles, we have so many misguided men and women. People may want to know the will of God for their lives but cannot know the will of God in and of themselves. In Jeremiah 10:23, we read this: "O LORD, I know the way of man is not in himself; it is not in man who walks to direct his own steps." That is, we just don't have what it takes to know God's will, in and of ourselves.

Let me give you some propositions, some principles from the story of Saul in Acts 9.

Principle 1. Guidance Is Promised

Guidance is promised. "Arise and go into the city, and you will be told what you must do" (Acts 9:6). You say, "That was to Saul so long ago. That's not necessarily a promise to me." Then let me give you a number of other verses:

"For we are His workmanship, created in Christ Jesus for good works, which God prepared beforehand that we should walk in them" (Eph. 2:10). This verse teaches we are His workmanship; that is, we've been saved by God's grace, created in Christ Jesus to do good works *which God prepared beforehand* that we should walk in them. The King James Version says, *"Which God hath before ordained* that we should walk in them." God has a plan ordained for us, before it ever comes to pass.

"The steps of a good man are ordered by the LORD, and He delights in his way" (Ps. 37:23). God orders your steps, one at a time—that's God's plan for you.

"I will instruct you and teach you in the way you should go; I will guide you with My eye" (Ps. 32:8).

What does this mean? When my children were little, while I was preaching, no one else would know it, but they would sometimes be misbehaving on the second or third pew. I could look at them while still preaching and say with my eye, "If you don't straighten up, you're going to get punished when we get home." Men, have you ever been in a restaurant, and you start a conversation, and your wife will look at you, and you know you're not supposed to go there? It is wonderful that we can have that same kind of intimate relationship with the Lord where He "guides us with His eye."

Think of other promises.

"The LORD will guide you continually" (Isa. 58:11). That's a solid promise.

Or, "In all your ways acknowledge Him, and He shall direct your paths" (Prov. 3:6). What a wonderful promise.

What God said to Saul was not just to this one individual. Thank God, there is a like promise to us as well. I have a Father above me who is controlling all things. I have a Savior beside me directing my footsteps. I have the Holy Spirit within me, energizing me and impressing my heart, my mind, and my will.

Now, having said that about guidance and God's will being promised, I want you to learn some things about God's will.

God's Prevailing Will

First, there is His great overarching sovereign, or *prevailing,* will. God can never ever be ultimately thwarted in His purpose. No matter what you do, say, or think, God's sovereign will is going to be done. Not a blade of grass moves without His controlling power; not a raindrop falls but what He is over it all. "There are many plans in a man's heart, nevertheless the LORD's counsel—that will stand" (Prov. 19:21).

God's Permissive Will

There is not only God's prevailing will; there is God's general or *permissive* will. For example:

"The Lord is . . . not willing that any should perish" (2 Pet. 3:9).

"For this is the will of God, your sanctification" (1 Thess. 4:3).

"I will therefore that men pray" (1 Tim. 2:8 KJV).

This is God's permissive will, but not everybody subscribes to God's permissive will. God in His sovereignty has granted to man a free will that he may also disobey God. "I call heaven and earth as witnesses today against you, that I have set before you life and death, blessing and cursing; therefore choose life, that both you and your descendants may live" (Deut. 30:19).

God's Personal Will

God has a will for each one of us. He has as many plans as He has people. God is interested in each individual. In fact, "the very hairs of your head are all numbered" (Matt. 10:30). "The steps of a good man are ordered by the LORD" (Ps. 37:23). God has a plan for my life, for your life, for everyone's life.

Let me sum it up this way:

- It is God's *prevailing will* that the kingdoms of this world will become the kingdoms of our Lord and His Christ. That's going to happen, hallelujah!

- It was God's *permissive will* that we make right choices. For example, Christians are not to marry unbelievers, but sometimes, tragically, they do.
- I believe it was God's *personal will* for me that I married Joyce. See, I believe that God brought Joyce to me and brought me to Joyce. I can remember when I would walk her home from church or school and then leave her at the doorstep, and all the way home I would be praying, "O God, let me marry that girl!" And He did.

God's Word teaches that God has a special plan, a specific plan, a personal plan for each one of us. He orders our steps and that's amazing. It would be like the president of the United States being interested in a barnacle on a piece of driftwood out in the middle of the Atlantic Ocean for God to be interested in us, yet He is.

He Knows Your Name

We have learned that model prayer, "Our Father which art in heaven, hallowed be Thy name . . ." The little boy prayed, "Father in heaven, how does He know my name?" He does; He knows your name. You're not an incident; you are not an accident. God deals with every one of us as individuals.

Principle 2. Guidance Is Provisional

Now here's the second principle: Not only is guidance promised, but guidance is also provisional. There are some biblical provisions if we would know God's will.

Willingness

You must be willing to know God's will. Remember what Saul said in Acts 9:6? "Lord, what do You want me to do?" Are you *really* willing to do the will of God? If not, you probably won't know it. Sometimes people want to build a house, and they already have in mind the kind of house they want. Maybe they've drawn it on a piece of paper at the kitchen table, and they get an architect. What they're asking the architect to do is not really to design a house from scratch. They're saying, "This is the kind of house I want. This is what *I want*—now design it."

I'm afraid we come to God sometimes like this. We say, "Lord, here's what I want for my life. Now God, You design a plan for my life." We're really just asking God to superimpose and conform His will to our will.

I heard about a vagabond who spent his entire life walking across the country from one end to the other. Somebody asked him, "How do you decide which way you're going to go?" He replied, "It really doesn't make any difference to me; I just go." And they said, "What do you do if you're walking down the road and you come to a fork in the road. How do you determine whether you're going to go this way or that way?" He said, "That's simple. I just pick up a stick and throw it in the air and whichever way it lands, that's the way I go." Then he said, "Sometimes I have to throw it up six or seven times for it to land right."

A lot of us are that way. We say, "Oh, you know I just want the will of God," but we keep throwing the stick up until it lands the way we want to go.

Are you really willing? Honestly ask yourself this question: "Do you really, sincerely, want the will of God?" There must be willingness.

Meekness

After Saul had met the Lord on the road to Damascus, the Bible says, "Then Saul arose from the ground, and when his eyes were opened he saw no one. But they led him by the hand and brought him into Damascus" (Acts 9:8). It is obvious that this once proud and arrogant Pharisee was now meek in spirit.

The Bible says in Psalm 25:9 (KJV): "The meek will he guide." Do you know what the word *meek* means? It means "a teachable and a broken spirit." In the olden days when the cowboys would take a wild stallion and break him, they would call that "making him meek." They didn't cripple him. They wanted to keep his strength. They wanted him to have fire and speed. But they wanted to be able to put a saddle and a bridle on that stallion.

Has God ever been able to put a saddle and bridle on you? Have you come to the place where you say, "Lord, what do You want me to do?" Is Jesus Christ truly your Lord? Are you meek and teachable? A boy sometimes will drop out of school when he's fourteen. He'll say, "They can't teach me anything." If that's his attitude, he is probably right; they can't teach him anything because he doesn't have a teachable spirit.

Openness

Saul asked the Lord, "*What* do You want me to do?" In other words, "I'm open." He doesn't say, "Now Lord, this is what I want to do; help me to do it." He's just open to God's voice. You see, God will speak, but you must hear His voice. Many times He speaks with a still, small voice, He doesn't shout (see 1 Kings 19:11–12). That's all the more reason we need to report for duty in the morning.

Do you have a quiet time? If God speaks with a quiet voice, you have to have a quiet time to hear it. If you're around a lot of furor and hubbub and noise, and somebody is whispering, you're not going to hear it. That's the reason you need to have a quiet time to say, "Lord, what is it that You really want me to do?"

Our prayer needs to be listening prayer as well as talking prayer. Have you ever had a conversation with a person who does all the talking? And you don't get to talk. They think they're having a conversation, but they're just making a speech. I'm afraid our prayer is like that sometimes. We say, "Listen Lord, Your servant speaks," rather than, "Speak Lord, Your servant listens."

Yieldedness

You have to yield to the will of God. It's not enough to know the will of God; it's not enough to hear God. You have to say, "Lord, I am ready to do Your will."

> Then Saul arose from the ground, and when his eyes were opened he saw no one. But they led him by the hand and brought him into Damascus. And he was three days without sight, and neither ate nor drank.
>
> Now there was a certain disciple at Damascus named Ananias; and to him the Lord said in a vision, "Ananias."
>
> And he said, "Here I am, Lord."
>
> So the Lord said to him, "Arise and go to the street called Straight, and inquire at the house of Judas for one called Saul of Tarsus." . . . And Ananias went his way and entered the house; and laying his hands

on him he said, 'Brother Saul, the Lord Jesus, who
appeared to you on the road as you came, has sent me
that you may receive your sight and be filled with the
Holy Spirit.'" (Acts 9:8–11, 17)

In this episode we learn that God sent a messenger to Saul to
instruct him. This man named Ananias learned from God that Saul
was a chosen vessel to spread the gospel. To read this story is to see
this proud Pharisee, Saul, now yield to instructions from a little
known disciple of Jesus. That is yieldedness.

If you are not willing to yield to the will of God, why should God
show you His will?

What For?

Imagine a man who comes into a service station with an old
automobile. All four tires are flat, the fenders are banged in, no
water in the radiator, no oil in the crankcase, the gas tank is rusted
through—it's just a crate. He pushes it right up to the pump and tells
the attendant, "Fill her up." The guy looks at that car and says,
"What?" He says, "Fill her up." The attendant would ask, "What
for?"

We say, "God, show me Your will," and God asks, "What for?"
What for if you're not yielded? If you're not ready to do the will of
God, why should God show you His will? Would you be willing,
yielded enough, to sign the contract at the bottom and say, "Now
God, You fill it in"?

If you take all these things together, you're going to know the will
of God for your life. You say, "Wait a minute. I can't sign the contract until I read it." Well, with another man I would suggest that's

wise business, but with God it's a lack of trust. Romans 12:1–2 says, "I beseech you therefore, brethren, by the mercies of God, that you present your bodies a living sacrifice, holy, acceptable to God, which is your reasonable service. And do not be conformed to this world, but be transformed by the renewing of your mind, that you may prove what is that *good and acceptable and perfect will of God.*" You may not know what it is, but I can tell you it's good, acceptable, and perfect. God promises that. He has a wonderful will for your life.

Principle 3. Guidance Is Practical

We Are Guided by the Miracles of God

God sometimes directs by miracles. That's not an ordinary way, but God does sometimes work supernaturally in visions, in dreams, in miracles. He directed Saul here by a miracle. Jesus appeared to him. There was a bright light, he was knocked down, and the Lord spoke to him in an audible voice. He's never appeared to me that way, but it is certainly possible. This is not the normative way. This is an exception that proves the rule of God's normal dealings, yet we dare not discount miracles.

We Are Guided by the Word of God

In Acts 9, in addition to speaking to Saul through a miracle, God spoke to him through His Word. "Then the Lord said, 'I am Jesus, whom you are persecuting'" (Acts 9:5).

Saul was already full of the Word of God. He had heard Stephen preach one of the greatest sermons ever preached just before this and was standing by when Stephen was stoned to death (see Acts 7). And now the Lord Himself was speaking to him.

Remember that Saul was a Pharisee, and he was steeped in the Word of God. All of this began to come together as the Word of God was speaking to this man. Much of the will of God for your life is found in your Bible.

Let me tell you something. Pay close attention. Never seek the will of God concerning something that God has clearly commanded or something that God has clearly forbidden. That's arrogance and dangerous. It is foolish and wicked to try to know the will of God apart from the Word of God. If God has said it in His Word, that is His will for you!

We Are Guided by the People of God

You're going to find out that God will use other people to help you to know His will for your life. "Now there was a certain disciple at Damascus called Ananias; and to him the Lord said in a vision, 'Ananias.' And he said, 'Here I am, Lord.' So the Lord said to him, 'Arise and go to the street called Straight, and inquire at the house of Judas for one called Saul of Tarsus, for behold, he is praying. And in a vision he has seen a man named Ananias coming in and putting his hand on him, so that he might receive his sight'" (Acts 9:10–12). God used Ananias to help Saul know His will.

Could it be that God is using me right now to help you? You may be used by God to help other people. You're often going to find the will of God in the context of a Christian church and with other believers in a wonderful way.

If you are getting instruction, encouragement, or guidance from a brother or sister, make certain that they are walking in the Spirit. God confirmed to Saul that this man who was coming, Ananias, was of Him. And God will confirm that to you.

Thank God for people who give us wise counsel. Proverbs 24:6 says, "For by wise counsel you will wage your own war, and in multitude of counselors there is safety." God is the final Counselor, and we have to obey God rather than men. But don't get so arrogant that you can't learn from other people.

We Are Guided by the Spirit of God

Another way you can know God's will is the Spirit of God. This is the inner witness. "And Ananias went his way and entered the house; and laying his hands on him he said, 'Brother Saul, the Lord Jesus, who appeared to you on the road as you came, has sent me that you may receive your sight and be filled with the Holy Spirit'" (Acts 9:17). Saul also found the will of God by the Spirit of God.

God's Holy Spirit does lead us. Another wonderful verse is Romans 8:14: "For as many as are led by the Spirit of God, these are sons of God." That's plain, isn't it? "Led by the Spirit of God." And Galatians 5:18: "But if you are led by the Spirit, you are not under the law."

So the Holy Spirit of God leads. And I love the phrase "led of the Spirit."

The Holy Spirit never shoves; He guides and leads. If you find a hand between your shoulder blades just shoving you, that's not the Holy Spirit. The Holy Spirit is gentle. I've met people who are compulsive and driven. They're not led people. They're generally religious zealots, and usually they're dangerous.

We are *led* by the Spirit of God. He guides; He doesn't shout. Remember the still, small voice. And it's so interesting how God leads like this, and it's so mystical.

But all of us have some wonderful stories to tell. I was supposed to go to a meeting in downtown Memphis, and I thought the man

147

I was to go with, another pastor, was going to stop by and pick me up. It dawned on me when he didn't come by my house that morning at 7:30 a.m., I was supposed to have been downtown at 7:30 a.m. on my own. It was a breakfast meeting; it was now too late to go. I can remember standing by my refrigerator like it was yesterday, saying, "Lord, what do You want me to do?" I prayed out loud, "It's too late to go to that meeting; what do You want me to do?" I felt impressed in my heart to take my wife, Joyce, to breakfast. Now here's the strange thing. I said, "All right Lord, I'll take Joyce to breakfast. Where should I take her?" I don't pray about where I go to breakfast normally. But I'm not just thinking this prayer; I'm actually verbalizing this prayer, talking out loud. No one else was in the kitchen but the Lord, and I said, "Lord, where shall I take her?" And I felt this impression, "Take her to the Holiday Inn at I-240 and Poplar." So I said, "Joyce, we're going to the Holiday Inn for breakfast."

We went there and were sitting in the window seat, having breakfast. An automobile drove up and parked in front. As he looked right through his windshield, there we sat. The man got out and came in. He said, "You are Adrian Rogers, aren't you?" I said, "Yes sir." He said, "I cannot believe this. You are the one man in all the world I need to see today." Then he told me a story about great trouble in his home, and he said, "Oh, my wife would trust you. Would you please talk to her today?" I said, "If you come by my house, I will."

Later that Saturday he and his wife came by my house. They prayed in my study and gave their hearts to Jesus. It was glorious. Those two people have been active members in our church for about two decades. They are wonderful, growing, godly people. I cannot help but believe that God, like a guided missile, put me right there in front of that plate-glass window that day. He said, "I can't believe this. You are the one man in all this city I need to see, and there you are." Well, God just simply said, "Go to the Holiday Inn, have breakfast."

Maybe if we all were walking in the Spirit, more things like that would happen. But they happen just enough to make us know that we ought to follow those sweet impulses of the Holy Spirit. And so I believe that the Spirit of God definitely leads us in mystical ways. Some people argue against that, but I'm enough of a mystic to believe that the Holy Spirit of God just directs us that way.

We Are Guided by the Wisdom of God

Notice in Acts 9:20–22: "Immediately he [Saul] preached the Christ in the synagogues, that He is the Son of God." Remember this man has just recently been a hater of Christianity and a persecutor of Christians, and right away he's a preacher! "Then all who heard were amazed, and said, 'Is this not he who destroyed those who called on this name in Jerusalem, and has come here for that purpose, so that he might bring them bound to the chief priests?' But Saul increased all the more in strength, and confounded the Jews who dwelt in Damascus, proving that this Jesus is the Christ." It's obvious that Saul is just infused now with a supernatural wisdom because he's filled with the Spirit.

The Bible says in Ephesians 5:15–18: "See then that you walk circumspectly, not as fools but as wise . . . understand what the will of the Lord is. And do not be drunk with wine, . . . but be filled with the Spirit." God gives wisdom. What is wisdom? Wisdom is seeing life from God's point of view. And when you get saved and when you are surrendered—walking in the Spirit and filled with the Spirit— you're going to find out you have the mind of Christ.

Don't be afraid to use your mind. Why would God renew your mind if He didn't want you to use it? We have the mind of Christ. The will of God is not found in getting wet around the lashes and warm around the heart and getting goose bumps and liver shivers. No, it is sanctified common sense. James said, "If any of you lacks wisdom, let him ask of God, who gives to all liberally and without reproach, and it will be given to him" (1:5). Get your motive clear and get your heart right, and then do what you think. Don't be afraid to use your mind. Dr. J. I. Packer said that "wisdom is the power to see and the inclination to choose the best and highest goal together with the surest means of attaining it." That's good! And so, James says, "If you need wisdom, ask God. God won't scold you for asking. God will give you wisdom."

We Are Guided by the Providence of God

In Acts 9, beginning in verse 23, you find out that when Saul is preaching Jesus, he runs into much difficulty. And by the way, Jesus didn't come to get us out of trouble—He came to get into trouble with us. And so now Saul is going to get into trouble. It doesn't mean that he's not in the will of God. Don't get the idea that if you get in the will of God it's going to be all honey and no bees.

"Now after many days were past, the Jews plotted to kill him. But their plot became known to Saul. And they watched the gates day and night, to kill him. Then the disciples took him by night and let him down through the wall in a large basket" (Acts 9:23–25).

I can just imagine this. Here's this great Saul—before all of this he was a big shot with the equivalent of three PhDs—and here he is in a basket being let down over a wall. You can imagine the humility of the thing, almost the ignominy of the thing, and yet he is in the will of God.

We're talking about the providence of God, and the point I'm making is this: There's a God who watches over the affairs of men. They planned to kill Saul, but God let him know of their plans. There's an unseen hand that guides—the providential hand of God.

Just Jesus!

Let me sum it up. I could take all these six practical principles and put them in one word. It's going to sound simplistic when I say it, but the will of God for you is Jesus. Just Jesus! This is not just pious talk. No, not at all! The church is the body, Christ is the head, right? Well, what is the will of my body? It is my head. I don't want my hand to have a will of its own. I don't want my hand to wake up this morning and say, "Good morning, Mr. Rogers, today I'm going to scratch your ear, put some food in your mouth, write some letters for you, and shave you." I don't want a hand like that, having its own plans and trying to serve me. No, the will of Adrian for his hand is his head. Who is the head of the church? Jesus.

Now friend, you take all of these things, whether the providence of God, the people of God, the Spirit of God, whatever it is, you just put one big overarching name over it, and it's just Jesus. Fall in love with Jesus and say to Jesus what Saul said to Jesus: "Lord, what do You want me to do?" He may use a lot of different ways to show you, but the will of God for your life is Jesus. He is Lord, He is the head of the church, and you surrender to Him.

Finally, let me give you three principles about the will of God:

- First—the will of God is for your welfare. It is not something you have to do; it is something you get to do. You would want the will of God if you had enough sense to want it, if you understood how much God loves you.

151

- Next, the will of God will never take you where the power of God and the grace of God cannot enable and keep you.
- And last, you are free to choose. God will not force His will upon you. You are free to choose His will. You are not free *not* to choose. You say, "Well, I won't choose." You just made a choice—you chose not to choose. You're free to choose, you're not free not to choose, and pay attention— you're not free to choose the consequences of your choice. You make a choice, and the choice chooses for you. You're free to jump out of a ten-story building; that's your choice. But then the choice chooses for you when you hit the ground. Do you understand what I'm saying? You're free to choose. You're not free not to choose. You're not free to choose the consequences of your choice.

And so what you really are is the sum total of your choices.

The wisest thing you can do and I can do would be to do what? Do what Saul did. Ask the first question, "Lord, who are You?" And second, "Lord, what do You want me to do?"

Every Christian Ought to Know

ABOUT FAITH AND HOW
TO HAVE IT

For the Scripture says, "Whoever believes on Him
will not be put to shame." For there is no distinc-
tion between Jew and Greek, for the same Lord
over all is rich to all who call upon Him.
For "whoever calls on the name of the LORD
shall be saved."
How then shall they call on Him in whom they
have not believed? And how shall they believe in
Him of whom they have not heard? And how shall

they hear without a preacher? And how shall they
preach unless they are sent? As it is written:
"How beautiful are the feet of those who preach the
gospel of peace, who bring glad tidings of good things!"
But they have not all obeyed the gospel. For Isaiah
says, "LORD, who has believed our report?" So
then faith comes by hearing, and hearing by the
word of God.

ROMANS 10:11–17

Imagine two letters dropped at the post office to be delivered. One letter is on crisp and expensive stationery. It is beautifully typed and elegant in language. However, it does not have a stamp.

Another letter is on cheap paper. It is written in pencil, smudged and filled with bad grammar and misspellings, but it has the right stamp.

Which letter will get delivered? The one with the stamp. It is not the eloquence and form of our prayers that gets them delivered but the stamp of faith.

Pray, believe; and you'll receive.
Pray and doubt; you'll do without.

If there were ever a time for us to have an earthshaking, mountain-moving, devil-defying faith in Almighty God, this is the time, this is the day, and this is the hour.

I don't know what you will accomplish in your Christian life, but I can tell you the measurement that will measure what you will accomplish. The Bible says this clearly and plainly, "According to your faith be it unto you" (Matt. 9:29 KJV). Not according to your fame. Not according to your feelings. Not according to your fortune. Not according to your friends. Not according to your fate. But according to your faith, be it unto you. Faith is the medium of exchange in the kingdom of heaven.

When you go to the grocery store to get groceries, you get groceries with dollars. But we receive from God by faith. Faith is heaven's medium of exchange. Faith is the greatest asset we have. Unbelief is the greatest stumbling block. Unbelief is the chief wickedness. Unbelief is the mother sin, the father sin, the parent sin. The sin of all sins is unbelief. Unbelief caused Eve to sin against God in the Garden of Eden. She failed to believe the Word of God. Unbelief locked the doors to the Promised Land; and the Israelites did not go in, the Bible says, because of their unbelief (Heb. 3:19). Unbelief tied the hands of Jesus when Jesus was in His own hometown. The Bible says, "He did not do many mighty works there because of their unbelief" (Matt. 13:58). The sovereign God has limited Himself to work according to the faith, the belief of the people of God.

What is the sin that sends people to hell today? It is not lying, it is not murder, it is not rape, it is not arson, it is not sexual perversion, it is not pride, it is not arrogance. It is unbelief! You see, Jesus died for all those other sins. Those sins have been paid for with His precious blood. The Bible says, "He who believes in Him is not condemned; but he who does not believe is condemned already, because he has not believed" (John 3:18). It is unbelief that shuts the door to heaven.

"If you can believe, all things are possible to him who believes" (Mark 9:23). And in the spiritual realm, if you do not believe, nothing is possible. The Bible says in the book of Romans that "the just shall live by faith" (1:17). Just as you live physically by breathing and from nourishment you take from food, you live spiritually by faith.

Think of all that comes to us by faith:

- Salvation—"Therefore, having been justified by faith, we have peace with God through our Lord Jesus Christ" (Rom. 5:1).
- The fullness of the Spirit—"That the blessing of Abraham might come upon the Gentiles in Christ Jesus, that we might receive the promise of the Spirit through faith" (Gal. 3:14).
- Victory over the world—"For whatever is born of God overcomes the world. And this is the victory that has overcome the world—our faith" (1 John 5:4).
- Victory over Satan—"Above all, taking the shield of faith with which you will be able to quench all the fiery darts of the wicked one" (Eph. 6:16).
- Sanctification—"Those who are sanctified by faith in Me" (Acts 26:18).

Think of all the problems that come when we fail to exercise faith:

- Worry—"God, I don't think You can handle this."
- Loneliness—God seems far away.
- Guilt—Our guilt gland is overactive because we do not trust God for cleansing. Faith is our acceptance of God's acceptance of us.
- Disobedience—If I truly believed God's Word, I would not violate it.

I pray that God will indelibly write the truths in this chapter upon your heart. Oh, the blessings of God that will come to you if you will learn to believe God.

It is absolutely necessary that you learn how to believe God. Consider with me the following factors that will help to build a vibrant faith.

The Reality of Biblical Faith

"Whoever believes on Him will not be put to shame" (Rom. 10:11). Faith must have the right object to be real faith. Sometimes people say, "Just have faith. Only believe." When a person says to me, "Just have faith," the first question in my mind is, Faith in what? They say, "Only believe." I ask, "Only believe what?" There is no power in faith alone. Don't think there's something mystical or magical about just believing. Your faith is no better than its object. Misplaced faith is dangerous. It is not faith that moves mountains. It is God that moves mountains. The Bible says in Mark 11:22: "Jesus . . . said to them, 'Have faith in God.'"

Many people think of faith as *positive thinking*. That's what people think faith is. Faith is not positive thinking. It will help you to think positively, and there's nothing wrong with positive thinking. But many people think there's something mystical and magical about "only believing." The reality of biblical faith in Romans 10:11 is that we are to believe *on him*. Your faith is no better than its object.

If you make faith simply positive thinking, do you know what's going to happen to you? You're going to get discouraged because there are going to come times when you're trying to think positively but you're not going to be able to think positively. A little boy came to his dad and said, "Dad, I think I flunked my math test today." His dad said, "That's negative thinking. You've got to be positive, son." To which the little boy replied, "I'm positive I flunked it!"

If you look into yourself and you're trying to think positively, actually you're going to find that rather than encouraging you it's going to discourage you. After a while it's going to dawn on you that you don't have what it takes, and you will be discouraged.

Don't Put Your Faith in Faith

If you put faith in faith, you're a sitting duck for the devil.

The devil will come to you and say, "You're not good enough to be saved."

You say, "I know it, but I don't have any faith in myself."

The devil says, "There are hypocrites in the church."

And you say, "I'm not putting faith in hypocrites. I'm trusting the Lord."

The devil will say to you, "But you don't feel like you should."

And you say, "I'm not trusting my feelings. I'm trusting the Lord."

You would think he'd go away. But do you know what he'll do? And this is the slyest thing of all. He'll say, "You say you're trusting the Lord, but how do you know your faith is strong enough? How do you know your faith is the real thing?" That's his dirtiest and most devious trick. Many people go under when Satan says this.

If the devil ever pulls that stunt on you, you just tell him, "Look devil, I am not putting my faith in faith; my faith is in Jesus." Now there's a difference in that. The least amount of faith in the right object is better than strong faith in the wrong object. We are to believe in Him.

Do you remember what the Bible says in Hebrews 12:2? We're to be "looking unto Jesus, the author and finisher of our faith." Looking unto Jesus. Don't look at your look. Don't put faith in your faith; put faith in God. The reality of faith is not positive thinking. It's not faith in faith. It is faith in God. Weak faith in the right object is better than misplaced faith in the wrong object. You ask, "Will God honor weak faith?" He certainly does. If He didn't, most of us wouldn't have anything from Him.

In Mark 9, there is a story about a man who had a little demon-possessed boy. He came to Jesus and said, "Lord, if You will, You can heal my boy." Jesus said to him, "If you can believe, all things are possible to him who believes." The Bible says, "Immediately the father of the child cried out and said with tears, 'Lord, I believe; help my unbelief!'"

And Jesus gave him just what he needed. He had a weak faith, but it was weak faith in God. I'm not saying we ought to have weak faith. It is far better to have strong faith.

Jesus told His disciples, "If you have faith as a mustard seed, you will say to this mountain, 'Move from here to there,' and it will be moved" (Matt. 17:20). What was He saying? The least amount of faith is greater than the greatest amount of difficulty, if it is faith in God.

If you want your faith to grow strong, don't put faith in faith. Put your faith in God. That's the way to have strong faith, to find out who God is.

If you want to cross a bridge and you don't know whether it could hold you up, you might be afraid and tremble and try to make yourself believe; you might screw up your courage and endeavor to believe so you can cross the bridge. That would be ridiculous. Just look at the bridge. It's made of concrete and steel, and semi trucks are going over it every day. When you see the bridge and understand what the bridge can do, then it's easy for you to cross the bridge.

When you see who God is, then rather than putting faith in positive feelings and putting your faith in faith, you put your faith in God, and your faith will grow.

Let me use another illustration. Up in the northern parts near the source of the Mississippi, it was a bitterly cold winter, and the Mississippi River had frozen over. There was a man who, rather than going to the bridge, decided he would walk across the frozen ice. He didn't see anyone else out there. It looked so crusty and so thick. He said, "I believe I can walk across. I won't have to take the journey down to the bridge," and this man began to walk across that river on ice. When he got a distance from the shore, he looked at the other shore and thought, *Maybe I ought not to be out here. Maybe this ice won't hold me up. If I fall through, they'll never know what happened to me. I'm a fool. What am I doing out here?*

And as he turned around to go back to the other side, he said to himself, "I better walk softly." Then he thought, *I better get down on all fours, so I won't put my weight in any one place.* Then he said to himself, "That's not enough. I better lie down and squirm across. I may go through the ice. What a fool I am. My wife will never know what happened to me." He began to whimper and cry, and then he heard it, a roaring, cracking sound. "Oh," he said to himself, "The ice is breaking; I'm a goner." He put his face down. He began to pray, "God save me; help me Lord." The noise got closer and closer—that rumbling and roaring—but the ice didn't seem to be breaking. He looked up, and there was a man with a team of horses with a wagon loaded with logs driving across that river. That was the noise he heard. When he saw that, he jumped up and brushed off the ice and took his stroll across the rest of the river.

Now what was the difference in these two men? The second man knew the ice. The reality of faith is based on a knowledge of God. "[One who] believes on Him will not be put to shame" (Rom. 9:33). Do you want to have strong faith? Don't try to make yourself believe. Get to know God.

"And those who know Your name will put their trust in You" (Ps. 9:10).

"The people who know their God shall be strong, and carry out great exploits" (Dan. 11:32).

That's the reality of biblical faith. Your faith is no better than its object. You must know God.

The Root of Biblical Faith

All true biblical faith is rooted not only in knowing God but in hearing from the God that you know. "How then shall they call on Him in whom they have not believed? And how shall they believe in Him of whom they have not heard? And, how shall they hear without a preacher?" (Rom. 10:14). Then in verse 17: "So then faith comes by hearing, and hearing by the word of God." In order to have faith, you must hear from God. You cannot know the will of God by guessing at it. This verse says that faith comes. You don't generate it; it comes. God gives faith. "For to you it has been granted on behalf of Christ, not only to believe in Him, but also to suffer for His sake" (Phil. 1:29). It is granted to us to believe. God gives faith.

No one can believe God unless God enables him to believe. And how does God enable you to believe? God gives you a word. Faith comes by hearing and hearing by the Word of God. Therefore, contrary to popular belief, you don't *name it and claim it.* God speaks, and you *believe it and receive it.* "Faith is the substance of things hoped for, the evidence of things not seen" (Heb. 11:1).

What does *hope* mean? Today it means maybe, or it means strong desire. That's the way we use *hope* today, but friend, the word *hope* in the Bible does not mean what our modern word means. *Hope* in the Bible means bedrock assurance based on the promise of God. That's what hope is. It means assurance mingled with anticipation. That's the reason the Bible calls the second coming of Jesus, the "blessed hope." That doesn't mean it's the "blessed maybe"; it's the "blessed assurance." How do we know? He said so. He's not here yet, but we know He's coming. How do we know? Because He has said so.

"Faith is the substance of things hoped for" (Heb. 11:1). You know what the word *substance* means. Actually the Greek word is much like our English word. *Substance* implies something beneath you that you can stand on. When you're living by faith, you're not walking around on eggshells and Jello®. Friend, faith is not Jello. Why? Because it is the substance of things hoped for, things that God has said. The root of faith is the Word of God. Faith comes by hearing the Word of God.

How does God communicate His Word? We already said you cannot have faith unless God speaks. Well, how does God speak? There are two words for *word* in the Greek language. One is *logos.* The *logos* we could say is the Bible, the written Word that tells of the living Word. The revelation of God, given in Christ, revealed in the Bible—that's the *logos.*

But there's another word that is translated *word,* and that is *rhema.* That's the word used here in verse 17. Faith comes by hearing and hearing by the *rhema* of God. Not the *logos* but the *rhema.*

What does the word *rhema* mean? It means an utterance. It means a spoken word. We could call it a word from the Word. You take the Bible—that's the *logos*; and as you're reading, the Bible begins to speak to you out of the Word of God. You get a *rhema* from the *logos*. You get an utterance from God, and God speaks to you, and you hear in your heart.

The preacher is only the mailman who delivers the letter, but God gives the message. It's not enough to hear a sermon. "How then shall they call on Him in whom they have not believed? And how shall they believe in Him *of whom* they have not heard?" (Rom. 10:14). Notice that phrase *"of whom."* The New American Standard Version gives it this way, "How will they believe in Him whom they have not heard?" Not "of whom," but "whom." You must hear God. You must get a *rhema* from God.

How does God speak? You're reading the Bible or you're praying, and God puts that portion in your heart. God says, "This is from me. It is all true, but this is specially from Me to you."

You say, "Well, He never speaks to me that way." Are you listening? Do you have a quiet time? Are you saturated with the Word of God? Are you ready to do His will? Do you want to hear Him? Are you reporting for duty? The root of faith is the *rhema* of God.

The Result of Biblical Faith

What is the result, the purpose of faith? What does biblical faith do? Faith is not getting man's will done in heaven. It is getting God's will done on earth. The result of faith is the will of God.

Notice I said you cannot have faith unless you hear from God. Do you know what you're going to hear when you hear from God?

You're going to hear the will of God. When God speaks, God is going to say, "This is what I want done, and therefore, I want you to believe it."

You cannot have faith for anything that's not the will of God. If it's not the will of God, there's no possible way that you can have faith for it. Why? Because faith is the gift of God. Faith comes from hearing the Word of God, and God's not going to give you a word on something that's not His will. And that's wonderful because God is in control. Don't think that you can just believe for whatever you want and have it.

The Midas Touch

If I had enough faith, could I turn my car into solid gold? Not unless God wanted it turned into solid gold. That keeps God in control. Do you remember hearing about King Midas? He wished that whatever he touched would turn to gold. He just loved gold, and so he got his wish. He said, "Now I'm going to be wealthy. Whatever I want will turn to gold." But when he went to eat his food, it turned to gold. He couldn't eat it. When he kissed his beautiful daughter, she was no longer a daughter that he could love. What he thought would be a blessing became a curse.

If you had unlimited faith, it would become the same curse to you. If you could just say, "I can believe and have whatever I want," you'd make a mess of things. It would put you in the driver's seat rather than God. The result of faith is that the will of God is done.

You say, "Oh, that means fewer blessings for me." No, it means *more* blessings for you because, as I said in chapter 7, the will of God is not something you must do; it is something you get to do.

"Now this is the confidence that we have in Him, that if we ask anything according to His will, He hears us" (1 John 5:14).

- What is the *reality* of faith? It is faith in God.
- What is the *root* of faith? You hear from God.
- What is the *result* of faith? The result of faith is that God's will is done.

The Release of Biblical Faith

How do you release faith? What do you do? How does it get down into private, personal experience? How are you going to release your faith today? True faith does more than merely believe. It obeys. If what you say you believe does not translate into action, you don't really believe it.

The word *believe* in our language comes from the Old English "by live." What we believe, we live by. The rest is just religious talk. Let me tell you what faith is. Faith is belief with legs on it.

You may say, "If I can't believe, then it's not my fault. It's God's fault because God didn't give me faith. You said no one can believe unless God speaks to him; and maybe God didn't speak to me, so it's not my fault."

Right before Romans 10:17: "So then faith comes by hearing, and hearing by the word of God," verse 16 says: "But they have not all obeyed the gospel." They heard, but they didn't obey. God spoke, but why didn't they obey? Why didn't they believe? Not everybody is a believer. A few verses later in this same passage: "But to Israel he says: 'All day long I have stretched out My hands to a disobedient and contrary people'" (v. 21).

God is speaking, but not everybody will obey the gospel. Not everybody will release his or her faith. God stretches out His hand, but there are people who are disobedient and contrary. They debate. They hear the Word of God and God speaks; the Holy Spirit says, "Yes, that is true," but they parade it past the judgment bar of their mind. They say, "I don't think I'll believe that."

You can believe if you want to. Unbelief never comes out of the head but out of the heart. "Beware . . . lest there be in any of you an evil heart of unbelief" (Heb. 3:12). But isn't faith a gift of God? Indeed. So is breathing. God gives air and God gives lungs, but you can smother if you wish.

Let me sum it up with some clear and practical advice to have a victorious faith:

- Be *saturated* with the Scriptures. Remember that faith comes by hearing from God.
- Be *dedicated* to the Savior. Remember that faith is no better than its object. It's not so much a great faith in God as it is faith in a great God.
- Be *separated* from sin. Unconfessed sin is a faith killer. Don't be disobedient and expect faith. Read Romans 10:21 again. If you are having difficulty with faith, try repentance.
- Be *activated* by the Spirit. Remember that old song, "Trust and Obey"? Remember we are to obey the gospel. Real faith is belief with legs on it. Get started!

9

Every Christian Ought to Know

HOW TO BE FILLED WITH
THE HOLY SPIRIT

*See then that you walk circumspectly, not as fools but as
wise, redeeming the time, because the days are evil.
Therefore do not be unwise, but understand what the
will of the Lord is. And do not be drunk with wine, in
which is dissipation; but be filled with the Spirit.*

EPHESIANS 5:15–18

I want you to imagine a man who has bought, for the first time in his life, a brand-new automobile. He's never driven before, never had an automobile, and what he does not understand is that it has an engine in it.

He is proud of his car. He invites his friends over and shows them how beautiful the paint job is, how soft the seats are. And he says, "See how nice this is, what a sleek automobile this is." But everywhere he goes, he has to push it. Sometimes when he is going downhill, he can get in and coast, but that doesn't excite him too much because he knows every hill that he coasts down he's got to push that thing up the next hill.

While he's proud of his automobile and in some ways grateful that he has it, in other ways he secretly wishes he didn't have it. Rather than being a blessing to him, it became a burden to him. Rather than it carrying him, he has to push it.

And then somebody says, "I want to show you something. See that thing. That's called an ignition key. Put it right in there and turn it. *Vroom!*" "What's that?" "That's a thing called an engine. Now take that lever right there and put it where it says 'D' and then press that pedal," and that automobile begins to surge forth with power. "Hey," he says, "This is wonderful, this is glorious, this is amazing. Why didn't somebody tell me before? Why didn't somebody show me about this before?"

You say, "That's foolish. Nobody could be that dumb." You're right, unless it is the Christian who does not understand the power of the Holy Spirit of God.

Many Christians don't understand that when they got saved, God put an engine in their salvation. I don't mean to speak disrespectfully about the Holy Spirit by calling Him an engine, but He is the dynamism, the power of our Christian life. Many people are somewhat proud of their Christianity, but it's almost a burden to them. Rather than it carrying them, they are pushing it. And they're just grinding out this matter of being a Christian because they have not made the discovery of the wonderful Spirit-filled life. Ephesians 5:18 has a command of God: "And do not be drunk with wine, in which is dissipation; but be filled with the Spirit."

When you are filled with the Spirit, it will turn the drudgery to dynamism. Rather than making your Christianity a burden, it will become an empowering blessing to you.

The Reasons for the Spirit-Filled Life

Your Obedience

Let's consider some of the reasons for the Spirit-filled life. Here's the first reason: your obedience. Read Ephesians 5:18 again, "Do not be drunk with wine, . . . but be filled with Spirit." This is a command; it's not a request. It's not a suggestion; it is a command to obey.

Suppose a minister staggers into his pulpit thick-tongued, bleary-eyed, and hair disheveled. Someone says, "I think the pastor is sick." Then someone else gets up closer and says, "He's drunk!" Tongues would wag; meetings would be called. But the same Bible that says don't be drunk also says be filled with the Spirit. It would be a greater sin for that pastor to show up not filled with the Spirit than it would be for him to show up drunk.

Now some may not believe that. But the Bible teaches that the sins of omission are greater than the sins of commission (James 4:17). It's a greater sin to fail to do what you ought to do than to do what you ought not to do. As a matter of fact, if you do what you ought to do, you can't be doing what you ought not to do because you can only do one thing at a time. A man who is filled with the Spirit is not going to be drunk in the first place. You could be sober and not Spirit-filled, however.

By the way, far more harm is done in our churches by people who are not Spirit-filled than by people who are drunks. Far more harm is done by people who are trying to do the work of God in their own flesh.

Now let's have a little language lesson. When the Bible says, "Be filled," that is in the *imperative mood.* When you want someone to do something and it's very important, you say, "It is imperative you do this." That means it is necessary. And it is in the *present tense.* It doesn't say, "Get filled," it says, "Be filled." The question is not, were you filled? The question is, are you filled? It is *plural in number*; it literally says, "Be *being* filled." The command is not just for the pastor, the evangelist, or the Bible teacher. It is for *every* person who is a child of God.

The command to be filled is *passive in voice.* That means we are acted upon. This is not something that we attain; this is not something that we earn. It is a gift of God. It is the Spirit of God who fills us. The Lord longs to fill every believer.

Your Obligations

The first reason for being filled with the Holy Spirit is obedience. It is imperative that you be filled with the Holy Spirit of God. Here's the second reason that you need to be filled with the Holy Spirit: not only your obedience but your obligations. So many people think, "If I just knew what I'm supposed to do, then I'd have it made." No, you also need the power to do what you know that you ought to do. It's one thing to know what God wants you to do, but you alone cannot do it. You need power to fulfill your obligations.

You Need to Be Spirit-Filled in Your Worship Life

Consider your obligations in your worship life. In Ephesians 5:19, the apostle Paul says, "Speaking to one another in psalms and hymns and spiritual songs, singing and making melody in your heart to the Lord." What's he talking about there? Worship! In order to worship as you ought to worship, you need to be filled with the Spirit of God. Jesus said we're to "worship the Father in spirit and truth" (John 4:23).

Have you ever been in a boring worship service? No, you never have. Perhaps you have been in a boring *church* service but not a boring *worship* service. Real worship is not boring; it is invigorating. But a service apart from the Holy Spirit of God—oh how "tedious and tasteless the hours." We wear the varnish off the bench trying to get out of a "dry as dust" church service. How sad to see a "filled church of empty people trying to overflow."

To keep worship from becoming routine and mundane, you need to be filled with the Holy Spirit of God.

You Need to Be Spirit-Filled in Your Wedded Life

You need to be filled with the Holy Spirit of God not only in your worship life but also in your wedded life. "Wives, submit to your own husbands, as to the Lord" (Eph. 5:22). In this day of militant feminism, that verse is politically incorrect. Some will say, "That makes the wife inferior to the husband." No, it doesn't. Everybody knows that a woman is infinitely superior to a man at being a woman. And a man is infinitely superior to a woman at being a man. God made us different that He might make us one.

The Bible teaches that a wife is to submit to her husband. Submission is one equal voluntarily placing himself or herself under another equal that God may thereby be glorified. It has nothing to do with inferiority or superiority. The Bible teaches that God the Son is in submission to God the Father (1 Cor. 15:28). God the Son is not inferior to God the Father. He has a name that is above every name. Yet there is even that line of authority in the Godhead.

In this day when people are standing up for their rights, how is a woman going to learn the spirit of submission? Only by being filled with the Holy Spirit of God.

This passage is not directed only to women. It applies to men as well. Look at Ephesians 5:25. Now he's talking to the husbands: "Husbands, love your wives, just as Christ also loved the church and gave Himself for her." How can a husband love his wife as Christ loved the church? Only when he's filled with the Holy Spirit.

Of which of the two partners does God require the most difficult task—the wife to submit or the husband to love? A more difficult task is required for the husband. He is to love his wife as Christ loved the church. Jesus *died* for the church! Now that is love.

- A husband is to love his wife *sacrificially* because that's the way Jesus loves the church.
- He is to love his wife *supplyingly*; that's the way Jesus loves the church.
- He is to love his wife *steadfastly*; that's the way Jesus loves the church.
- He is to love his wife *selflessly*; that's the way Jesus loves the church.

Most women don't mind being in submission to a man who loves her enough to die for her and shows it by the way he lives for her. But in his own strength, a man doesn't have what that takes. I don't have what it takes to do anything the way Jesus does. I can't love my wife as Jesus loved me, but Jesus *in me* can when I'm filled with the Holy Spirit.

You Need to Be Spirit-Filled in Your Work Life

Ephesians 6:5 says, "Bondservants, be obedient to those who are your masters according to the flesh, with fear and trembling, in sincerity of heart, as to Christ." Do you know what that means? Your employer in your secular job is the one you ought to obey. When you go to work in the morning, you are to serve your boss as if he were Jesus. You say, "Wait a minute! That two-legged devil? You mean I'm to serve him as if he were Jesus?" Read it in your Bible—black print on white paper—that's what it says.

Now that just cuts across the grain. In our society today the motto is, "Get all you can, can all you get, sit on the lid, and poison the rest." Many would say, "I don't give a hoot about my boss. I'm not going to serve that man that way! I'll serve Jesus, but I'm not going to serve him!" To the contrary, you are to serve Jesus by serving him. Why do you do that? That may be your greatest testimony. Your job becomes your lampstand to let your light shine, and it becomes your temple of devotion.

Do you know what an employer ought to say when he calls the employment agency? "I need some helpers, and by the way, if you have any Christians down there, send them over first. They get here on time, they don't steal, they don't gossip, they work with industry, and in their relationship they must think I'm God. If you have any more Christians, send them over." If Christians would begin to live like that on Monday, would others believe what is taught on Sunday?

It is not human nature to live that way. How can you live that way in your work life? Only if you are filled with the Holy Spirit of God.

You Need to Be Spirit-filled in Your War Life

In Ephesians 6:12, Paul is still talking about the Spirit-filled life. He says, "For we do not wrestle against flesh and blood, but against principalities, against powers, against the rulers of the darkness of this age, against spiritual hosts of wickedness in the heavenly places." You're in a battle, and your battle is a spiritual battle. You're not wrestling with flesh and blood. Your enemy is not the IRS, not your mother-in-law, not the Democrats, not the Republicans, not your neighbor, not your boss; the devil is your enemy. "We do not wrestle against flesh and blood, but against principalities, against powers, against the rulers of the darkness of this age, against spiritual hosts of wickedness in heavenly places." Therefore, it is a spiritual battle, and unless you're filled with the Holy Spirit, you're going to lose that battle. The Bible teaches that when we're filled with the Spirit, "He who is in you is greater than he who is in the world" (1 John 4:4). The devil laughs at our schemes, he mocks at our organizations, he ridicules our good intentions, but he fears the Spirit of God in a holy Christian. So in your war life, you need to be filled with the Spirit of God.

You Need to Be Spirit-Filled in Your Witness Life

In your witness life you need to be filled with the Spirit of God. In Ephesians 6:19, Paul is asking them to pray—all of this is in the context of being filled with the Spirit—and he says, "And for me, that utterance may be given to me, that I may open my mouth boldly to make known the mystery of the gospel." Paul was an intellectual, he was a world traveler, he had a great mind, but he knew as every preacher knows that "all is vain unless the Spirit of the Holy One comes down."[1]

Before I preach, I pray because anything I can talk you into, somebody else can talk you out of. But what the Holy Spirit of God gives you is different. That's the reason the apostles said, "We are His witnesses to these things, and so also is the Holy Spirit whom God has given to those who obey him" (Acts 5:32). Do you know what I want? When I'm sharing, I want the Holy Spirit to say, "That's right! You listen to him. He's telling you the truth." I'm a witness, but so is the Holy Spirit to those that God has given to them that obey Him.

You have obligations in your worship life, in your wedded life, in your work life, in your war life, and in your witness life. And friend, in yourself you do not have the ability to live that kind of life. The Christian life is a supernatural life, and because of your obligations, you need to be filled with the Holy Spirit.

Your Opportunities

Ephesians 5:16 tells us to "redeem the time, because the days are evil." These are evil days. Do you know what they call for? Spirit-filled people. There's never been a greater opportunity to share the gospel than you have in this day and age. People have tried everything and nothing has worked, and they're looking one more time to the church and asking, "Is this real?" You and I need to buy up these opportunities and literally redeem the time.

Every day that you live without being filled with the Spirit is a wasted day. Jesus said in John 15:5, "Without Me you can do nothing." Do you know what nothing is? That's a zero with the edges trimmed off. You say, "I think I can do something." And I say that's your opinion. Jesus says it is splendid nothing. And we have such opportunities today that demand Spirit fullness. So many of us just think of a Spirit-filled life as a tonic to remove all stress.

A Spiritual First-Aid Kit

I heard of a lady who took a course in first aid. They were having testimonials about first aid, and she stood up and said, "I want to give a testimony. The other day out in front of my house, there was an automobile accident. An old man driving his car lost control, went over the curb, and hit an oak tree head-on. He was thrown out into the street. His skull was fractured, he had compound fractures in his limbs, and he was pumping his life's blood out on the asphalt." She said, "It was horrible, but I remembered my first aid. I remembered if I would put my head between my knees I wouldn't faint."

That's the kind of Christianity a lot of people desire. We just want to put our head between our knees and say, "Oh, I'm so glad I'm a Christian, so I can live in this horrible world." It is a horrible world, and our Lord has put us here as His representatives. Opportunities to serve Him are everywhere.

The Requirements of the Spirit-Filled Life

How can you be filled with the Spirit? It is not your responsibility to persuade God to fill you with the Spirit. So many people think, *If I could just persuade God to fill me with the Holy Spirit.* No, it is not your responsibility to persuade God to fill you with the Spirit but to permit Him to do so. God *wants* to fill you with the Spirit. He longs for you to live with power and victory. Let me give you three requirements for being filled with the Holy Spirit of God.

Requirement 1. Complete Commitment

We need to bow to Him in full surrender. Notice that I said *Him.* The Holy Spirit is a person. Don't get the idea that the Holy Spirit is an influence or quality of some kind. He is a person. That doesn't mean He has a body; it means He has personality. When I say personality, that doesn't mean that He is charming to be around, though He is. It means He thinks, He wills, He loves, He acts. Never call the Holy Spirit "it." Call Him the Holy Spirit and use the personal pronoun *He.*

Jesus said, "When He has come, He will convict the world of sin . . . of righteousness . . . and judgment" (John 16:8). You wouldn't say concerning me, "*It* wore a blue blazer." You would say instead, "*He* wore a blue blazer." I am a person. The Holy Spirit is a person. To be filled with the Spirit means to be occupied by a person.

Don't get the idea that you are some sort of a vessel and that the Holy Spirit is being poured into you or that the Holy Spirit is pouring something into you, like love or power. No, you are a temple, and He is a person. "Do you not know that your body is the temple of the Holy Spirit who is in you, whom you have from God, and you are not your own" (1 Cor. 6:19). Think of the Holy Spirit as a person who wants to come and take complete control of your body, which is His temple.

Make Yourself at Home

Suppose you have recently moved into a new house with a beautifully decorated guest suite. When your first guest comes to visit, you say, "I'm so glad that you came to my house today. I just want you to be at home. Come, let me show you. Here's your room. Here is your bath; here's where the towels are. Come in here; this is the kitchen; there's the refrigerator. I'm going to work; just help yourself." Maybe you have another car, and you say, "Here's the key to the second car; just come and go. Here's the key to the front door. I'll be gone for a while; just make yourself at home. My house is your house."

Suppose you do that, and you're sincere. And then you come home one evening, and you don't see your guest anywhere. You go into your bedroom, and there he is in your bedroom, sitting down at your private desk, the one that has the roll top on it. And he's rolled that top back, and he's going through your bank account, and reading your old love letters, reading your will, reading your personal diary.

You clear your voice, trying not to act irritated, and you say, "May I help you? What are you doing here?" And he says, "No, I don't need any help. Hey, I sure thought you made a lot more money than this. And you wrote some goofy letters." You start to feel the heat rising, and you don't know how to say what you are really feeling because this is a friend. You've invited him into your house.

But you say, "Pardon me, I don't know how to say this, but I really don't appreciate your going through my personal things like that. Would you please put that material down?" And he would say to you, "I don't understand you. Didn't you say for me to make myself at home? Didn't you say this was my house? Didn't you say nothing was off bounds? Boy, these sure are funny letters that you wrote." And you say, "But I didn't mean that. Now close that desk and please leave my room." And a cold chill fills the room.

I wonder sometimes if we don't do the same thing to the Holy Spirit. We say, "Holy Spirit of God, just take control of my life. Lord, here I am. I'm just turning myself completely, totally over to You."

Is there any area of your life that is out of bounds to the Holy Spirit? Your financial life, your sexual life, your personal life, your ambitions—anything, anywhere? To be filled with the Spirit means that there is a person who is completely occupying the temple of your life. Every room, the key to every closet, to every desk drawer, belongs to Him. That's what it means to be filled with the Spirit. It means a complete commitment. You just turn over the keys to Him.

Requirement 2. Continual Control

Many times people make a commitment to be filled with the Spirit but fail to understand what Ephesians 5:18 says, "*Be* filled." It is present tense, continual action. I am *being* filled. Notice the contrast. He says, "Don't be drunk, but be filled." Why didn't he say, "Don't steal, but be filled"? Why didn't he say, "Don't commit adultery, but be filled"? Why didn't he say, "Don't tell lies, but be filled with the Spirit"? Why did he say, "Don't be drunk with wine, but be filled with the Spirit"?

First, he's talking *in contrast.* Being filled with the Spirit is in contrast to being drunk. Being drunk is the devil's substitute for being filled with the Spirit.

But not only is he speaking in contrast; he is also speaking *in comparison* because being drunk is a lot like being filled with the Spirit. When a person is drunk, he is under the control of another influence; and therefore his speech, his thought patterns, his walk, everything is changed. A man who might be typically timid thinks he can whip everybody in the bar when he's drunk. A man may give away all of his possessions when he's drunk. He may enter into commitments, get married when he's drunk, and then spend the next several years repenting. When a man is drunk, he's dominated by another influence. What Paul is saying is, "By comparison, don't be drunk, but be filled with the Spirit. Let my Spirit come and control your walk, your talk, your speech, your thought habits. Be *filled* with the Spirit of God."

Think further about the comparison. How does a man get drunk? By drinking, right? How does he stay drunk? He has to keep drinking. Likewise, it's not enough to be filled with the Holy Spirit of God; you have to *keep being filled* with the Spirit of God.

The Scripture literally says, "Be *being* filled." It's not something where you say, "Well, that's done; what's next?" No, I know too many Christians who were once Spirit-filled and now they've "sobered up." We are to be *being filled* with the Holy Spirit of God.

It begins with complete commitment where you say, "Lord, here are the keys to every room; take control of my life." It results in continual control where you are *being filled.*

Requirement 3. Conscious Claiming

Being filled with the Spirit is a complete commitment, continual control, and a *conscious claiming.* You just claim the Spirit of God. How did you get saved? You claimed Christ as your Savior. You can get filled the same way. It's not a matter of feeling; it is a matter of filling. You just by faith say, "Lord, take control of my life."

Once you have made a complete commitment, you have fully surrendered every key, then you have every right to claim heaven's throne gift. Remember that God desires to fill you and has promised to do so. Jesus said concerning the Holy Spirit, "If anyone thirsts, let him come to Me and drink" (John 7:37).

Suppose you are in the desert dying of thirst and someone offers you a tall glass of cool water and says, "Drink." Then you say, "Yes indeed, water is wonderful. That's what I need. I am so thirsty," but you don't drink.

Many Christians, for whatever reason, fail to appropriate what our Lord has offered. Remember how you claimed salvation? You did it by faith. Do the same with the Spirit-filled life.

The Results of the Spirit-Filled Life

We've looked at the reasons and the requirements for being Spirit-filled. Now, let's look at the *results* of being Spirit-filled. Ephesians 5:18–21 says, "And do not be drunk with wine, in which is dissipation; but be filled with the Spirit, *speaking* to one another in psalms and hymns and spiritual songs, *singing* and making melody in your heart to the Lord, *giving* thanks always for all things to God the Father in the name of our Lord Jesus Christ, *submitting* to one another in the fear of God." Look at the words that end in –*ing*. In verse 19, *speaking* and *singing*; in verse 20, *giving*; and in verse 21, *submitting*. If you remember your English grammar, these words are called participles.

The participles mentioned in this passage are the *results* of a Spirit-filled life, and they deal with the three relationships that all of us have in life:

- We have a relationship to God.
- We have a relationship to circumstances.
- We have a relationship to other people.

In Your Relationship to God—a Spirit of Adoration

When you're Spirit-filled, what is going to be your relationship to God? You're going to be speaking and singing in worship. In your heart, in your life, when you're Spirit-filled, there will be a Spirit of adoration. "God is Spirit, and those who worship Him must worship in spirit and truth" (John 4:24).

Do you know how you can tell if you're Spirit-filled? You'll just be saying all day long, "Jesus, I love You, I love You." When you get in the car, you want to sing songs to Him, you want to praise Him, you want to lift your hands. You find the love of God just pouring out of you. Your life is a temple, and a temple is for praise. You're just going to be praising the Lord.

I tease about not being able to sing, but I tell you, I get in the car and roll up the windows and sing to Jesus. I don't let anybody else hear, but He'd just as soon hear me sing as you because He put that song in my heart.

So when you're Spirit-filled, there will be a spirit of adoration—a burning, blazing, passionate, emotional love for Jesus Christ.

In Your Relationship to Circumstances—a Spirit of Appreciation

Notice Ephesians 5: "Giving thanks always for all things to God and the Father under the name of our Lord Jesus Christ." A Spirit-filled Christian is not grumbly hateful; he's humbly grateful. He is giving thanks—not sometimes but always—for all things. And friend, there's no way that you can do that apart from being filled with the Holy Spirit of God.

When you praise God in evil circumstances, that doesn't mean that you approve of evil; it means that you trust in God. It means that you know that no matter what happens, God is greater.

In Your Relationship to Others — a Spirit of Accommodation

Notice again verse 21: "Submitting to one another in the fear of God." A Spirit-filled Christian is one who has learned to accommodate himself to other people. He submits to other people. Submission is not for women; it is for Christians. "Submitting to one another in the fear of God."

You hear a person say, "I know my rights!" Well, what right does a dead man have? We're crucified with Christ. Show a person his rights, and you have a revolution. Teach him his responsibilities, and you'll have a revival. You and I need to learn to love other people and to submit to one another in the fear of God. I don't submit to you because of you; I submit to you because of Jesus. And you submit to me the same way. Oh, how wonderful to be around Spirit-filled brothers and sisters who have learned the spirit of accommodation.

A Personal Question

May I ask you a personal question? I'm going to ask this, so you might as well say yes. Are you filled with the Spirit? Are you right now consciously filled with the Spirit of God?

This is not simply a request. It is a command to obey. Be filled with the Spirit. And when you are filled with the Spirit, do you know what you're going to find? That beautiful automobile has an engine, and the ignition key is faith to believe the Word of God.

10

Every Christian Ought to Know

HOW TO DISCOVER HIS
SPIRITUAL GIFT

*Having then gifts differing according to the grace
that is given to us, let us use them: if prophecy, let
us prophesy in proportion to our faith; or ministry,
let us use it in our ministering; he who teaches, in
teaching; he who exhorts, in exhortation; he who
gives, with liberality; he who leads, with diligence;
he who shows mercy, with cheerfulness.*

ROMANS 12:6–8

Recently it was Joyce's birthday. I bought her a gift, and I wrapped it. I got the paper; I got the ribbon. I folded, stuffed, searched, found a bow, and put it on top. It really looked good—so good, in fact, she didn't believe I wrapped it! But I did wrap it, and I took great joy in putting that gift, beautifully wrapped, on our kitchen table so she could come and see it. Then I had joy watching her as she unwrapped her gift.

You Are a Gifted Child

You may have never thought about it this way, but as a member of God's family, you are a gifted child. God has wrapped up a gift in you.

You may say, "I'm not gifted; I'm just a lowly servant. I'm not even worthy to lead in silent prayer in the children's department."

Although you may feel unworthy and ungifted, you *are* gifted. God is the One who gives the gift. Don't come with some false humility and say that you do not have a spiritual gift.

Alexander the Great, the conquering general, once gave a beautiful and priceless golden cup to a lowly servant. When the servant saw the gift, he said, "Oh, no, that's too much for me to receive." And Alexander drew himself up and said, "It is not too much for me to give."

What if I had put that gift on the table for Joyce with a card, and she didn't even bother to unwrap it—just left it there and would not even unwrap the gift? I would have been disappointed, and she would not have had the joy of receiving what I gave to her. At the judgment seat of Christ, you will give an account of what you did with your spiritual gift—the stewardship of your spiritual gift. You need to discover your spiritual gift, so we're going to learn about how to unwrap it.

In the Christian world we've often divided people up into the clergy—those who are in full-time ministry—and the laity—the ones in the pew. A little girl was asked to define and describe the clergy and the laity. She said, "The clergy are paid for being good; the laity are good for nothing."

What I want to do is to help you not to be good for nothing but to be good for something. You may not realize it, but if you're saved, you have been called into the ministry. God has a ministry for all of us and each of us. Even your secular job can be your temple of devotion and your lampstand of witness.

You are a gifted child. I want to help you to unwrap your spiritual gift.

Start Unwrapping

Are you one who says, "I'm frustrated. I don't seem to be making any progress in my Christian life. I don't see any victory, and I don't have any joy"? And I ask, "What are you doing for Jesus?" "I'm going to church on Sunday morning. I'm sitting there. I'm listening to music. I'm singing songs and listening to my pastor preach."

Your problem is that you need to find a ministry. You need to discover your spiritual gift and put it to work for your Lord. There are three kinds of people in every church—those who make things happen, those who watch things happen, and those who don't even know anything is happening. Most are the watchers, the observers, who have never really gone to work.

We come to church, sit in our pews, listen to messages, and call that the service. The service ought to begin when we leave the building. Someone once said that the average church is like the people at a football game. Down there on the field are twenty-two men desperately in need of rest, and up there in the stands are fifty thousand people desperately in need of exercise. That's what we have in the church.

If you are tired of just drawing your breath and drawing your salary, if you are not content to sit around and endure until you die, then here is great news. God has called you to serve Him, and God has equipped you to serve Him. God has given to you a spiritual gift. You're to take that gift, discover it, develop it, and deploy it for Jesus.

The Description of the Gifts

Now concerning spiritual gifts, brethren, I do not want you to be ignorant.

1 CORINTHIANS 12:1

Paul says that you have a grace gift, and he says, "I don't want you to be ignorant concerning gifts," yet the average Christian and the average church is saturated with ignorance when it comes to spiritual gifts.

These gifts are *spiritual* gifts. In verse 4 they are called in the Greek *charismata. Charis* is the Greek word for *grace.* They are grace gifts, or "gifts of the Spirit."

I'm not talking to you about *material* gifts but *spiritual* ones. If I were to ask you, "Who wants to be a millionaire?" you'd probably perk up and say, "Yeah, I want to be a millionaire." I'm talking to you about something far more valuable, but the devil may have clouded your mind.

I'm not talking about material gifts, nor am I talking about *natural talent.* A spiritual gift is not a natural talent; it is supernatural ability. All talents are from God, but talents are not unique to the saved. Unsaved people may be very talented. We will see that spiritual gifts are supernatural enablements given to God's children for service to Him. A spiritual gift may be linked to a natural talent, but it goes beyond natural talents. It is not merely natural; it is supernatural. A Christian is naturally supernatural.

The description of the gifts is that they are spiritual gifts. They are not earned. They are not learned. They are the supernatural gifts of grace.

The Distortion of the Gifts

You know that you were Gentiles, carried away to these dumb idols, however you were led. Therefore I make known to you that no one speaking by the Spirit of God calls Jesus accursed, and no one can say that Jesus is Lord except by the Holy Spirit.

1 CORINTHIANS 12:2–3

Notice next that these gifts may be distorted. Evidently, there was a lot of spiritual craziness going on in Corinth. Corinth was a carnal church. Paul says, in effect, "Look, let's get rid of this ignorance. There are all kinds of strange things happening here. Spiritual gifts are being distorted."

Do you know what the devil wants to do? The devil wants to give the Holy Spirit a bad name. The devil wants to take something that is good and distort it and pervert it. By the way, the devil is a pervert. The devil has no raw material; God made everything. So anything that is bad is a perversion of that which was once good. The devil wants to take spiritual gifts and distort them.

Carried Away

We see this happening today in America. Someone says, "Have you heard about the revival going on in thus and such a place? All kinds of strange things are happening. People are falling down and being, as it were, glued to the floor; some of them indecently exposed, some of them laughing, out of control. Some roaring like lions and barking like dogs. "Hallelujah, revival has come!"

That's the way some people in Corinth were. They were "carried away." They were led away by "these dumb idols." Some would get worked up to such a frenzy they would even call Jesus accursed.

Let me tell you something about real revival. Real revival is never manifested by the gifts of the Spirit. Real revival is seen by the fruit of the Spirit, which is "love, joy, peace, longsuffering, kindness, goodness, faithfulness, gentleness, and self-control" (Gal. 5:22–23). Real revival doesn't put you out of control. Real revival brings you under the control of the Holy Spirit. Sometimes people say, "I was just carried away. I couldn't help it." They had better read 1 Corinthians 14:32: "The spirits of the prophets are subject to the prophets." I've been in services sometimes where somebody would disturb the service and say, "God just came on me." No. "The spirits of the prophets are subject to the prophets." And, again, Paul says in 1 Corinthians 14:40: "Let all things be done decently and in order."

Let's Magnify Jesus

Anytime you find worship that draws away from the Lord Jesus Christ, even worship that seems to magnify the Holy Spirit rather than the lordship of Jesus, that worship is contrary to the Bible. No one can say that Jesus is Lord but by the Holy Ghost. Jesus, speaking of the Holy Spirit, says, "However, when He, the Spirit of truth, has come, He will guide you into all truth; for He will not speak on His own authority, but whatever He hears He will speak; and He will tell you things to come. He will glorify Me, for He will take of what is Mine and declare it to you" (John 16:13–14).

Any movement or any teaching that has the Holy Spirit for a figurehead is distorted. I love the Holy Spirit. He lives in me. I rejoice in the dear Spirit of God, and I can say with Isaiah, "The Spirit of the Lord GOD is upon Me, because the LORD has anointed Me to preach" (61:1). When you see a parade, you'll never see the Holy Spirit leading that parade. If it's a spiritual parade, you'll see Jesus leading the parade and the Holy Spirit standing on the sideline saying, "Look at Him, look at Him, look at Him."

You don't go beyond Jesus to the Holy Spirit. That's foolishness. Friend, you'll never go beyond Jesus. You may go deeper into Jesus, but you'll never go beyond Jesus. And don't let anybody come to you with teaching that distorts spiritual gifts and takes away from the glory of the Lord and Savior, Jesus Christ. "And He [Jesus] is the head of the body, the church, who is the beginning, the firstborn from the dead, that in all things He may have the preeminence" (Col. 1:18).

Do you want to know whether any church is Spirit-filled, whether any preaching is Spirit-filled, whether any music is Spirit-filled, whether your gift is operating? Ask, "Is it giving preeminence to Jesus Christ?" That's it. Don't let your gift be distorted.

The Diversity of the Gifts

There are diversities of gifts, but the same Spirit.
There are differences of ministries, but the same
Lord. And there are diversities of activities, but it
is the same God who works all in all.

1 CORINTHIANS 12:4–6

Let's think about the diversity of the gifts. What does the word *diversities* mean? Just different kinds. In verse 4 you find the word *gifts,* in verse 5 the word *ministries,* and in verse 6 you find the word *activities.* Do you see it—gifts, ministries, and activities?

- The gifts speak of God's *provision.* God has given you a gift.
- Ministries speak of God's *purpose.* God has given you a gift for a purpose.
- And activities—the word we get our word *energy* from— speak of God's *power.* Your gift needs power to operate.

God makes a provision. God has a purpose for that provision, and God gives you power so that you might fulfill the purpose of that provision that God has given you. So there is a diversity of gifts, but it is the same Holy Spirit who gives them. What we have is unity in diversity.

Many couples here in America are given gifts when they get married. It's a custom. They are given waffle irons, blenders, toasters, can openers, coffeemakers. And these gifts have different functions, and they have different capacities, but if they use electrical power, they have to be plugged in. They don't operate without the power. It's the same power that operates them all, yet they all have different functions and different capacities.

And that's what Paul is saying about the body of the Lord Jesus Christ. We have different capacities, we have different functions, but it is the same Spirit. And what you need to do is plug in your spiritual gift by being filled with the Spirit.

Diversity in a church is not bad; it is good. Division is bad. Unity is good.

And what is unity?

- Unity is not *unison*. A choir sings in unity but not necessarily in unison. They may sing different parts; that's what makes it beautiful. God doesn't want us all to be alike. We're not a congregation of clones. God makes us different to make us one.

- Unity is not *uniformity*. Everybody is not doing the same thing. Uniformity comes from pressure from without. Unity comes from life from within. We all share the same Holy Spirit.

- Unity is not even *union*. You say, "We're all members of the same church." That's union but not necessarily unity. Having all the corpses in one graveyard is not going to cause unity. No. It is the unity of the Spirit. Let's celebrate our different gifts in the church; they are a source of unity. They all come from the same Holy Spirit.

The Design of the Gifts

But the manifestation of the Spirit is given to each one for the profit of all.

1 CORINTHIANS 12:7

What is God's design concerning these gifts? What purpose does God have for your spiritual gift? "For the profit of all." Your gift is meant to profit the entire body. Your gift is not for selfish purposes. It is not an end in itself but a means to an end.

Your spiritual gift is not for your *enjoyment*; your spiritual gift is for your *employment*. Your spiritual gift is a *tool,* not a *toy.* It is to bless the church body.

God gives you a spiritual gift that you might do a job and to get that job done in the church of the Lord Jesus Christ. My gift is going to bless you. Your gift is going to bless me. We're going to bless one another. Phillips translates it this way: "Each man is given his gift by the Spirit that he may use it for the common good." It's not some introverted, self-centered gift. Spiritual gifts are designed for *mutual encouragement.* Quit asking, "What's in it for me?"

God wants you to be a blessing to your church and, therefore, to make your church a blessing to your community and to make your community a blessing to the world.

The Distribution of the Gifts

For to one is given the word of wisdom through the Spirit, to another the word of knowledge through the same Spirit, to another faith by the same Spirit, to another gifts of healings by the same Spirit, to another the working of miracles, to another prophecy, to another discerning of spirits, to another different kinds of tongues, to another the interpretation of tongues. But one and the

*same Spirit works all these things, distributing to
each one individually as He wills.*

1 CORINTHIANS 12:8–11

Let's think next about the distribution of the gifts. How are they distributed? They're distributed by the Holy Spirit who gives them.

You don't decide this. He sovereignly decides. He chooses the gift for you. There is no need for you to ask God for a particular spiritual gift. If you're saved, He's already given you the gift. Your gift was a birthday gift; it came on the day of your spiritual birthday, when you were born again.

My brown eyes came with me when I was born, and that's a natural characteristic. Your spiritual gift is a supernatural characteristic, and it came when you were born again. It is your joy and responsibility to discover the gift and develop the gift that God has already given you.

When the Holy Spirit came into you, He didn't come in empty-handed; He came in with a gift. "As each one has received a gift, minister it to one another, as good stewards of the manifold grace of God [charisma of God]" (1 Pet. 4:10). Every believer has received that gift.

Have you ever watched a little baby discover his hands? It's amazing. He comes with those hands. You never go to the hospital and say, "Now put the hands on." He comes with those. But there comes a time when a child just discovers those little hands. Your spiritual gift came when you were born again. It is a birthday present—learn to use it.

Let's look at some of the gifts the Holy Spirit has distributed. There are two primary places in the Bible where spiritual gifts are listed: 1 Corinthians 12:8–10 and Romans 12:6–8. These passages are not an exhaustive listing of spiritual gifts, but they are illustrative and helpful.

At this point I am going to blend these lists and categorize them. I think it may help to clarify and simplify the subject. Later you may want to do an exhaustive, verse-by-verse study.

I have broken the list into three basic categories. To some degree they may seem arbitrary, but I believe it will give insight as you seek to discover your gift.

- Teaching/Leadership Gifts
- Service Gifts
- Sign Gifts

Teaching/Leadership Gifts

The following gifts are practical, needed, and more common in the church. Scan the list and see if you seem to resonate with one or more of them.

Leadership (Rom. 12:8)

It is not the motivation to be a big shot but to coordinate things; to help people see the big vision; to move them toward that vision; to coordinate the activities of others for a common goal, for the glory of God. It is the gift to preside, to lead, to stand before others. A person who has this gift also has the gift of vision. He sees where we ought to go, and he begins to lead and motivate people in that direction.

Prophecy (1 Cor. 12:10; Rom. 12:6)

What is prophecy? Prophecy is the ability to speak for God. It is not merely foretelling, though some of that is included. It is forthtelling. It is speaking the Word of God. Some have the gift of prophecy. And, as a matter of fact, in chapter 14, Paul says this is a gift greatly to be desired among the church.

There is much misinformation about prophecy. Some people today claim to have the office of a prophet. No, the office of a prophet is no longer. The church is built on the foundation of the apostles and the prophets. You don't keep laying the foundation every story. The foundation was laid two thousand years ago. We build on it. I think we may be putting the finishing touches on the roof.

But there *is* the gift of prophecy. What is this gift? I hear some people say, "My gift is prophecy," and they think they are anointed by God to tell other people off. No, that's not what the gift of prophecy is. As a matter of fact, quite to the contrary. Read 1 Corinthians 14:3: "But he who prophesies speaks edification and exhortation and comfort to men." That's not telling folks off. To edify is to build up. To exhort is to fire up. To comfort is to shore up and to hold up. That's what a prophet does, and that's what is needed so much in the church today. There's the gift of prophecy, and I thank God for it.

Teaching (Rom. 12:7)

If you have this gift, you want to clarify truth. You'll have a desire to search out things and validate truth that's been presented. You'll have a questioning mind and you'll be used in Bible classes, neighborhood Bible studies, backyard Bible schools, and so forth. You may use that gift as a mother. I believe my precious daughter, Janice, has that gift, and she uses it with her own children.

Exhortation (Rom. 12:8)

What is exhortation? That's the desire and ability to stimulate people in their faith, to encourage them to love Jesus more. If you have that gift, you're going to enjoy personal counseling. Perhaps you will be in the music ministry. You may be used in witnessing and outreach, going after those who are lost, strayed, or far from God. Thank God for the exhorters and encouragers.

Wisdom (1 Cor. 12:8)

What is wisdom? It's not just being intelligent. It is not mere common sense. It is uncommon sense. Wisdom is seeing life from God's point of view. Certain people have the gift of godly wisdom, and these are the kind of people I go to when I want guidance or insight. People who have the gift of wisdom make wonderful counselors.

Discerning of Spirits (1 Cor. 12:10)

And then he mentions the gift of the discerning spirits. We need to learn that not everything that is spiritual is of God. There is spiritual wickedness, and demons are masters of deception. The discerning of spirits is a greatly needed gift in the church of our Lord today. Because the devil has come with so much counterfeit flimflam, we need some with the gift of discerning. It's not the ability to go around and judge who is saved and who is lost. That's not your prerogative to do that, and Matthew 7:1 warns against that. But thank God for those who can pull away the devil's cloak of deception.

Service Gifts

May the dear Lord give us more people with the gifts of service. Too many are enamored with success rather than service. Jesus' life was marked by service. That ought to give dignity to the service that some feel too important to do.

Ministry (Rom. 12:7)

This is another word for service. And you're going to find yourself, if that is your gift, doing what so many people do—meeting spiritual needs in a practical way. Think of the service done through this gift in the church—these wonderful ushers, the nursery workers, those who drive the buses, those who keep the church grounds, those who work in maintenance, those who work the sound system. That's the gift of ministry, or service.

Giving (Rom. 12:8)

We're all commanded to give, but some people have the gift of giving. They are motivated to entrust personal assets to others so that the work of God may be carried on. They make good decisions to meet immediate needs. They're careful in their giving, but they're willing to give. They have the ability to accumulate and disperse assets.

Faith (1 Cor. 12:9)

When Paul talks about faith there, he's not talking about saving faith and serving faith common to all Christians. The Bible says, "God has dealt to each one a measure of faith" (Rom. 12:3). This speaks of superabundant faith, the *gift* of faith. You read about it in the next chapter. "Though I have all faith, so that I could remove mountains" (1 Cor. 13:2). If God wants you to move mountains, He'll give you mountain-moving faith. Not all of us have mountain-moving faith. I like to be around people who have mountain-moving faith. Thank God for some people who have that kind of faith. I know some people who are gifted with that kind of faith.

Take Away the Fog

If you want a blessing, read about George Mueller of Bristol, England, who lived in the nineteenth century. He had incredible faith. He raised millions of dollars to feed orphans, without ever asking anybody—just telling God about his needs. The story of his life is incredible. Here's one episode that I remember reading.

Mueller was on a sailing ship, going to Newfoundland, where he was supposed to speak. Unexpectedly, the ship stopped in the middle of the ocean. Mueller asked the captain, "Why is this ship stopped?" He said, "We can't move because of the fog." Mueller said, "But I've got to be there. I've got a speaking engagement. I've never missed a speaking engagement. It's God's will for me to be there." The captain said, "I'm not going to move this ship until the fog lifts." Mueller replied, "Very well, let's go to the chartroom and pray that God will take away the fog." The captain later said he went with Mueller just to humor him. Mueller got down on his knees and said, "God, the captain says he'll not move this ship until the fog is gone. I've got an appointment, and we need to move this ship. Father, in Jesus' name, take away the fog. Thank you, Lord." The captain said, "I started to pray," and Mueller said, "No, don't you pray." He said, "Why not?" Mueller said, "Two reasons. Number one, you don't believe He's going to do it; number two, He's already done it." As the captain later gave the story, he said, "I got up and looked, and the fog was gone!" Now that's a gift some people have. Not everybody has that kind of faith, but thank God for those who have the spiritual gift of faith.

Mercy (Rom. 12:8)

Maybe this is your gift. Oh, how needed that is. What is the gift of mercy? It is to identify with people and comfort people who are in distress. One of the things I know that my wife has is the gift of mercy. She's always reminding me of the needs of other people. And if you feel empathy and sympathy for the misfortune and heartaches of others, and then mentally, emotionally, and practically relate to those needs, that may be your gift. And you'll find yourself in hospital visitation, benevolence, counseling, and other acts of mercy.

Sign Gifts

Sign gifts were given to authenticate the work of apostles and prophets, particularly at the beginning of a new age (dispensation) when God does something new and different in the world.

Knowledge (1 Cor. 12:8)

A person with this gift doesn't know everything. Nobody knows everything. Nobody knows one-tenth of 1 percent of everything, but some have a gift of knowledge. Literally, in the Greek language, it is a "word of knowledge," just as in law you might have a word of law or a point of law.

This is the ability to know things that you could not know other than by divine intuition or revelation. It is not something that's learned from school. It is God-given insight. The devil counterfeits this gift, and by the way, the devil counterfeits all of these gifts. The counterfeit of this gift is what we call clairvoyance. Yet there is a gift of knowledge whereby one can know things by divine revelation that he could not know any other way. For example, how did Simon Peter know that Ananias and Sapphira were lying in Acts 5? He said,

"You've not lied unto men but to the Holy Ghost." How did Peter know that? He had the word of knowledge. God just told him that.

I think God has given me, sometimes, a little insight into this. I was preaching one time in a revival meeting. In the middle of the sermon, someone came down the aisle of the church, found a man on about the third row, tapped him on the shoulder, and led him out. The man happened to be the sheriff. I said, "There goes the sheriff. Most likely there's been an automobile accident and liquor has been involved, and somebody's been killed." Well, why would I say that? I had no knowledge about what had happened.

Later that night there was a knock on my motel door. That sheriff came and said, "I need to get saved." And he said, "Do you remember what you said about the wreck and its cause? I went out there and an automobile had hit a logging truck head-on, and the driver was killed. When I looked in the automobile, there was a broken whiskey bottle. The man who was killed was the man that ran against me for sheriff of this county." He said, "I need to get saved." He did get saved. I believe the Holy Spirit was at work when I said what I did in the church service.

Now I don't think knowledge is my gift. I think that was just a blip on the horizon of my spiritual world. I don't have the gift of knowledge, but I think I understand something about how that gift works.

Healings (1 Cor. 12:9)

"Now, Adrian, do you believe God heals?" Absolutely. God heals by miracle, and God heals by medicine. God heals instantaneously, and God heals in time. And God heals by doctors. Thank God for doctors, for Jesus said, "Those who are well have no need of a physician, but those who are sick" (Mark 2:17). And, yes, there is a supernatural gift of healing. The apostles had the gift of healing.

I don't know anybody today who has the gift of healing. I'd like to meet someone who says he does. I wouldn't put him on stage somewhere and let selected people come by. I'd take him to the hospital, to the children's ward, and see whether he has the gift of healing.

I believe the hottest part of hell is reserved for people who merchandise people's maladies and sicknesses and pains with some charlatan act of healing. I believe in healing, but oh, may God have mercy on those who make merchandise of other people in this particular area.

When Jesus died, not only did He take your sins, but He also took your sickness. And the Bible says, "By His stripes we are healed" (Isa. 53:5), but we're waiting for the redemption of the body. Read Romans 8. That has not yet come, but it will come. Hallelujah! Nonetheless, the gift of healing is listed. If God raises up someone today with that gift, I will rejoice, but the Spirit gives gifts "as He wills." The gift of healing does not seem normative in this age.

Miracles (1 Cor. 12:10)

Miracles normally came in clusters in the Bible. There were miracles, obviously, around the creation, miracles around the ministry of Moses, miracles around the ministries of Elijah and Elisha, miracles with Jesus and the apostles, and there will be end-time miracles. And I am certainly not opposed to miracles. I don't know anybody today who has the gift of miracles, but I would not deny God's ability in that area.

I don't think miracles would be effective in bringing the lost of Jesus. As a matter of fact, Jesus had to rebuke the miracle mongers of His day who followed Him, not because of who He was but because of what He did. But I'll share with you a verse that is a wonderful verse to me: John 10:41–42 speaks of John the Baptist. Was John the Baptist filled with the Holy Spirit? You'd better believe it. The Bible says he was filled with the Spirit from his mother's womb. But now, listen to this. "Then many came to Him and said, 'John performed no sign [miracle], but all the things that John spoke about this Man were true.' And many believed in Him there." It wasn't some miracle that John did that brought people to Jesus. It was Jesus that John preached. I would rather have it said about me that many believed on Jesus through my word than that I had the power to do miracles. I mean that with all of my heart because that is the lasting miracle, the new birth, the greatest miracle of all. God, however, may give to any He chooses the gift of miracles.

Tongues (1 Cor. 12:10)

What is the gift of tongues? It is the ability to speak in a language one has not learned. It is not an unknown language but a known language. The word that is translated *tongue* is the Greek word *glossa,* and it means "a recognizable language."

In the first mention of tongues in the New Testament, men heard these tongues and recognized them as their native language (Acts 2:8).

To have this gift is not a sign that one is Spirit-filled. As a matter of fact, tongues are not a sign to God's people about anything. Tongues are a sign to the unsaved. "Therefore tongues are for a sign, not to those who believe but to unbelievers" (1 Cor. 14:22).

The sign that one is filled with the Holy Spirit is not speaking in a tongue or language he does not know but to control the one tongue he has. I'm serious. See what Paul says in 1 Corinthians 13:1–2. The fruit of the Spirit is love (Gal. 5:22).

The primary purpose of this gift was to authenticate the ministry and message of the apostles. Many believe it was a temporary sign gift.

Interpretation of Tongues (1 Cor. 12:10)

Everybody in the body is to profit from the use of a gift. Suppose some foreign, unconverted Jews visited the early assembly of believers. Someone would then stand and praise God in a language he had not learned, but these foreigners understood because it was their native tongue. They would be amazed and convicted.

But what about the others in the church? They wouldn't understand the foreign language without an interpreter. There must then be someone with the gift of interpretation so all are edified, and no one is left out. Tongues and interpretation must work together.

Discovery of the Gifts

Finally, let's think for a moment about discovering our gifts. Paul in Romans speaks about discovering spiritual gifts.

A Matter of Lordship

I beseech you therefore, brethren, by the mercies of God, that you present your bodies a living sacrifice, holy, acceptable to God, which is your reasonable service.

ROMANS 12:1

Realize you are not your own. Be willing to be a living sacrifice. Consecration is not giving God anything. It is taking our hands off of that which already belongs to Him. Such a sacrifice is to be voluntary, total, and irrevocable.

A Matter of Stewardship

And do not be conformed to this world, but be transformed by the renewing of your mind, that you may prove what is that good and acceptable and perfect will of God. For I say, through the grace given to me, to everyone who is among you, not to think of himself more highly than he ought to think, but to think soberly, as God has dealt to each one a measure of faith.

ROMANS 12:2–3

When you make this sacrifice, your mind is transformed. Your transformed mind will recognize God at work in you. You have a new mind to think with and will more easily recognize your gift. True humility says, "I am what I am by the grace of God."

Don't insult God by saying you don't have a grace gift. True humility is not denying God's gift. To deny your grace gift is not humility but unbelief and rebellion. To fail to use your grace gift is a tragic waste. It is poor stewardship of the gift entrusted to you. One day you will answer to the Lord concerning the stewardship of your gift.

A Matter of Membership

For as we have many members in one body, but all
the members do not have the same function, so
we, being many, are one body in Christ, and indi-
vidually members of one another.

ROMANS 12:4–5

We belong to Jesus and to one another. It is in the context of the body that the various members discover their function. A hand severed from the body is not only useless but also grotesque.

Gifts are best discovered in the fellowship of the church. Get active in the church, and your gift will come to the surface. Let me mention four principles that seem to operate in the context of active membership.

When you learn to accept yourself, be yourself, and give of yourself to the fellowship, you're going to discover your gift. You are naturally supernatural.

Enjoyment

You will have a sense of doing what feels natural. There will be a corresponding fulfillment in your heart and mind.

Encouragement

Others in the church will recognize your giftedness. For example, the mouth has no problem recognizing the hand that feeds it. Conversely, it is sad to see someone who thinks he has the gift of preaching when no one else has the gift of listening.

Enablement

The God who calls is the God who enables. Your gift may be latent. Early on I could not conceive of myself as speaking and writing, but as I moved out in ministry, God gave me special help "and I thank Christ Jesus our Lord who has enabled me, because He counted me faithful, putting me into the ministry" (1 Tim. 1:12).

Enlightenment

There is the mystical part of it all. The Holy Spirit will say "amen" in your heart to help confirm your gift and ministry. You will have the sense of cooperating with the Lord. As a part of the body, you will receive impulses from the Head.

Bill Gothard tells this classic illustration. He imagines a party, and they're getting ready to serve the dessert. The person bringing the beautiful dessert to the table trips, and the dessert falls on the floor. There is the episode. Now here's how the different gifts may come into practice. The person who has the gift of prophecy says, "That's what happens when you're not careful." A person who has the gift of mercy says, "Don't feel bad; anybody could do that." A person who has the gift of service says, "Hey, let me help you clean it up." A person who has the gift of teaching says, "The reason it fell is it was too heavy on one side. Next time put it in the middle." The person who has the gift of exhortation says, "From now on, let's just serve the dessert first, and put it in the middle of the table so it won't fall." The person who has the gift of giving says, "I'll buy a new dessert." And the person who has the gift of administration says, "Jim, get the mop. Sue, please help pick it up. Mary, you go fix some more dessert."

That's a great illustration. You see how all of these different gifts are necessary and how they all work together.

You are a gifted child. God doesn't want you to go to church just to sit and soak. Your life is going to be meaningless, to a degree, until you discover your spiritual gift, and put it to work.

11

Every Christian Ought to Know
HOW TO PRAY (WITH POWER)

In this manner, therefore, pray: Our Father in heaven, Hallowed be Your name. Your kingdom come. Your will be done on earth as it is in heaven. Give us this day our daily bread. And forgive us our debts, as we forgive our debtors. And do not lead us into temptation, but deliver us from the evil one. For Yours is the kingdom and the power and the glory forever. Amen.

MATTHEW 6:9–13

Praying with power! There's not a more important subject in all the world for a Christian than to learn how to pray. Not only to learn *how* to pray but to pray *with power,* to pray in the Spirit, to pray to get prayers answered. As Christians we must realize that nothing lies beyond the reach of prayer except that which lies outside the will of God. Prayer can do anything that God can do, and God can do anything!

In Matthew 6:9–13, our Lord shows us how to pray. Notice, He did not say, "Pray this prayer." He said, "In this manner, therefore, pray." This is not a prayer simply to be repeated mindlessly. Sometimes at a gathering in a civic auditorium, someone may say, "Now let's just all stand and say the Lord's Prayer." This is not necessarily appropriate.

In the first place, many of these people may not even be Christians, and they have no real right, as we're going to see in a moment, to call God their Father. Second, we do not just stand and say a prayer. Prayers are not meant to be said; they are meant to be prayed. You might ask, "What's the difference?"

Suppose I were to come to your house and sit in your living room, and you said to me, "Say a conversation." That would be silly. Prayer is talking with God, not merely repeating words. Jesus said we are not to pray with vain repetition. The key is in Matthew 6:9, "In this manner, therefore, pray." This is a guide to show us how to pray. Pray like *this!*

I confess there may be times when the words of this prayer fit my need perfectly. Then I may want to repeat word for word what our Lord taught here. But I am not merely repeating words; I am praying out of my heart to our great God using *His* words.

Learning How to Pray

For many Christians the major failure in life is failing to learn to pray. There is no sin in your life that proper prayer could not avoid. There is no need in your life that proper prayer could not supply that need. That is why I emphasize that nothing lies outside the reach of prayer except that which lies outside the will of God. What fools we are if we do not learn to pray!

It is important that we look at the model prayer in Matthew 6:9–13 that our Lord gave us. Here He tells us how to pray.

The Persons of Prayer

Look in Matthew 6:9 which says, "In this manner, therefore, pray: Our Father in heaven, Hallowed be Your name."

Who are the persons in this prayer? A child and his Father. We're coming to God and speaking to God, as our Father. It is important to understand this because real, powerful prayer—prayer that prevails—is for the children of God.

You might say that this is to be taken for granted because everybody is a child of God. No, they're not! *Not* everyone *is a child of God.* Jesus said to the unsaved Pharisees, "You are of your father the devil, and the desires of your father you want to do" (John 8:44).

Who are the true children of God? The Bible says in the first chapter of John, concerning the Lord Jesus, "But as many as received Him, to them He gave the right to become children of God, to those who believe in His name" (1:12). So not everybody is a child of God—only believers!

The Children of God

Often we hear people speak of the universal fatherhood of God and the universal brotherhood of man. That is not right. God is not universally the Father of all, and all people are not necessarily brothers. We may be brothers in our humanity, but spiritually we are not brothers until we are born into the family of God and have one common Father. God becomes our Father when we are born into the family of God.

Some may argue that since God created us that He is the Father of us. Well, God also created rats, roaches, buzzards, and rattlesnakes. He's not their Father! No, He does not become the Father by creation; He *becomes the Father* by new birth.

The first thing that must occur if you want your prayers to be answered and you want your prayers to be powerful is to become a child of God. In order to be a child of God, you must receive the Lord Jesus Christ as your personal Savior. Have you done that? Does Christ live in your heart? If so, then you are ready to pray.

When you can say, "Father," you'll see how easy it is to pray.

Sometimes I have asked people to pray, and they say, "Oh, I'm sorry, I can't pray." And these people are professing Christians! Why can't they pray? Surely they can talk to an earthly father. Anyone who can talk to an earthly father can talk to their heavenly Father. You do not have to be an amateur Shakespeare in order to pray. You do not have to pray in old English, or convoluted terms, or poetic meter. You can just talk to God out of your heart. That's the way a child talks to his father.

Suppose, when my children were living at home, my daughter came to me and said, "Hail thou eminent pastor of Bellevue Baptist Church. I welcome thee home from thy sojourn. Wouldest thou

214

grant to thy second daughter Janice some money that I may sojourn to yonder apothecary and procure for myself some cosmetics to adorn my face?" That would have been ridiculous, wouldn't it?

This is the scenario that would more likely have happened: "Daddy, I love you. It's so good to have you home. Daddy, I need some money. I need to get some things at the drugstore." She would have spoken to me out of her heart because I am her father. Now that doesn't mean that she would be disrespectful to me. It does not mean that we are to be irreverent to God either. We can speak to God right out of our hearts and say to Him, "Father."

Galatians 4:6 says, "And because you are sons, God has sent forth the Spirit of His Son into your hearts, crying out, 'Abba, Father.'" The word *Abba* is an Aramaic word, a diminutive term. The best translation is "Daddy."

Have you ever thought about calling the great God—the One who scooped out the seas and heaped up the mountains and flung out the stars, who runs this mighty universe—have you ever thought about calling Him, "Daddy"? Would that be irreverent? No.

God's Spirit in our hearts cries out "Abba, Father" if you have been born into the family of God. If you have been born into the family of God, you can spiritually crawl up into His lap, put your arms around His neck, and talk to Him, as you would to your own father.

Some people think they have to pray through a priest or a saint. They illustrate this by using the example of talking to the president. They say you would not go directly to the president; you would go to your senator or congressman. Then he would go to the president for you. They surmise from this scenario that you cannot go directly to God, but you can go to the priest or saint who then goes to God for you.

Well, my friend, I am not going to go through my congressman if the president is my daddy. If the president is my own dear father, I'm not going to say, "Mr. Congressman, will you tell Dad something for me?" Not if the president is my father.

You can go directly to God, your Father, if you are born again by faith in the Lord Jesus Christ as your personal Savior and Lord.

The Purpose of Prayer

Matthew 6:10 says, "Your kingdom come. Your will be done on earth as it is in heaven." Prayer has one purpose and one purpose only. And that is that God's will be done.

Prayer is not an exercise where we bend God's will and make it fit our will. Too many people have the notion that prayer is talking God into doing something that He ordinarily would not want to do. This is not true. Prayer is seeking the will of God and following it. Prayer is the way of getting God's will done on earth.

Some say, "I knew there must be some catch to it. All I get to have is the will of God. I don't want it if I don't get what I want." If you're thinking this way, let me tell you that God wants for you what you would want for yourself if you had enough sense to want it. God's will is *best* for you. God's will is not something that you *have* to do. God's will is something that you *get* to do.

God loves you so much. All good things will He give to those who walk uprightly in Him. God longs to bless you. God yearns to bless you. You must come to the place where you can know the will of God. Successful prayer is finding the will of God and getting in on it. You are not *hemmed in* by the will of God; you are *freed up* by the will of God.

The Bible says, "Now this is the confidence that we have in Him, that if we ask anything according to His will, He hears us"

(1 John 5:14). We must pray according to the will of God. But what is His will?

Some things are plainly stated in the Scriptures as God's will. For instance, the Bible says that the Lord is "not willing that any should perish" (2 Pet. 3:9). Obviously when a person is saved, God desires that sanctification because the Bible says, "This is the will of God, your sanctification" (1 Thess. 4:3).

While we know that certain things are the will of God, in other matters we must seek His will. Should you move to another city to take that new job? Should you sell your home? Should you go to this college or that college? Should you marry this boy or that girl? In all matters, if we seek the will of God, we will come to know the will of God.

How can we know the will of God? Jesus said, "If you abide in Me, and My words abide in you, you will ask what you desire, and it shall be done for you" (John 15:7). Now notice He says, "If you abide in Me, and My words abide in you." To "abide" is to lean upon Jesus moment by moment—to look to Jesus and depend upon Jesus. It also means that we are to read the Word of God daily, allowing it to move from the written pages into our hearts. Then the Holy Spirit shows us *how* to pray and *what* to pray. This is what the Bible calls praying in the Spirit.

The Holy Spirit in us helps us to pray. We pray *to* the Father, *through* the Son, and *in* the Spirit. If we surrender to the Spirit of God and abide in Christ, then His Word abides in us. Therefore, we can pray for whatever we will. Because strangely and wonderfully, what we now will is what He wills because we now have the mind of Christ. As we pray, we think the thoughts of Christ after Him.

One of the sweetest lessons I ever learned about prayer is this: *the prayer that gets to heaven is the prayer that starts in heaven.* What we do is just close the circuit. God lays something upon our hearts to pray for, we pray for it, and it goes right back to heaven.

Prayer is the Holy Spirit finding a desire in the heart of the Father and then putting that desire into our hearts and then sending it back to heaven in the power of the cross. Isn't that beautiful! And so what is the purpose of prayer? "Your kingdom come. Your will be done." We are to seek the will of God in all of our praying. That does not mean fewer blessings for us; it means more blessings.

The Provision of Prayer

Matthew 6:11 says, "Give us this day our daily bread." The Lord is telling us that in a practical way He will provide for our needs. One of the greatest verses in all of the Bible is, "My God shall supply all your need according to His riches in glory by Christ Jesus" (Phil. 4:19).

It does not say, "My God shall supply all your wants," because there are times when we want things we do not need. There are also times when we need things we don't want. My dad used to say, "You need a spanking." He was right. I *needed* one, but I didn't *want* one.

God will supply all of our needs and more according to His riches. It does not say *out* of His riches. A millionaire may give you ten dollars out of his riches, but that's not necessarily *according to* his riches. But my God shall supply all of our needs according to His riches in glory by Christ Jesus. We can come and say, "Father, give me today my daily bread."

This verse does not imply that all we can ask for is bread. We have many needs. That's the reason I was careful to point out to you at the beginning that this is not a prayer to be mechanically repeated. It is a model prayer. Jesus did not say, "Pray this prayer." He said, "Pray in this manner."

If you need bread, ask God for a loaf. If you need a job, ask Him for a job. If you need a house, ask Him for a house. Let the Holy Spirit show you what to ask for and then pray in the Spirit that your needs are met. I am convinced that many Christians do not have their needs met—when God desires to meet those needs—because they cheat themselves by failing to pray.

In James 4:2, we read that "you do not have because you do not ask."

When I was in college, I pastored a little country church on the Atlantic side of Florida, near the Indian River. It's a beautiful spot where some of the best citrus fruit in all of the world grows. When I was getting ready to return to college, I went down there and ran into one of the deacons. He had two big canvas bags filled with oranges, grapefruit, and tangerines. He said, "Adrian, this is for you." I said, "I can't eat all those oranges; they'll spoil." He said, "Take them back to college and give them away."

I put them in the trunk of my car, drove back to college, and put them in a closet. A day or two later, I was eating lunch and looking in the backyard when I saw a little boy sneaking around. He never knew I was watching him, so I decided that I would see what he was up to.

I saw he was going to steal an orange from a tree in my backyard. The orange tree was what we call a sour orange tree—an ornamental fruit, not meant to be eaten. He plucked one and ran away. I didn't have any extra money in those days, but I really believe I would have given a dollar to see this little boy take the first bite of that bitter orange.

But here is the irony of this example. Had that little fellow just come and knocked on my door and said, "Mister, may I have one of those oranges?" I would have said, "No son, you cannot. But if you'll come up here, I'll load you down with oranges." I had oranges that I was longing to give. That is what the Bible means by "we have not because we ask not."

One of these days when we are up in heaven, the Lord may take us by a great big closet, open the door, and say, "Look in there. You see all those things? Those were yours. They are provisions I made for you, but you wanted the devil's sour oranges, and that's what you got." You had not because you asked not.

This is the provision of the prayer: "Give us this day our daily bread."

The Pardon of Prayer

Matthew 6:12 says, "And forgive us our debts, as we forgive our debtors."

- Sometimes prayer is not answered because we are not praying to God as a Father. We have never been saved.
- Sometimes prayer is not answered because we are not praying in the will of God. We're not saying, "Your kingdom come, Your will be done." Instead, we're saying, "My kingdom come and my will be done."
- Sometimes our prayers are not answered because they are not asked. We simply do not say, "Father, give me what I need."
- And then sometimes our prayers are not answered because there is unconfessed, unrepented sin in our lives.

Along with asking for what we need, we need to remember that one thing we may need is forgiveness. That is why our Lord taught us to pray, "And forgive us our debts as we forgive our debtors."

I want to give you two prayer promises. Here is the first one. "If I regard iniquity in my heart, the Lord will not hear" (Ps. 66:18). And the second is, "Behold the LORD's hand is not shortened, that it cannot save; nor His ear heavy, that it cannot hear. But your iniquities have separated you from your God; and your sins have hidden His face from you, so that He will not hear" (Isa. 59:1–2). Not that He *cannot* hear; it is that sin has come between you and a Holy God. If we regard iniquity in our hearts, the Lord will not hear us.

Scripture does not say if you have sinned the Lord will not hear you. If that were the case, He would not hear any of us. Because we know what the Word of God tells us about ourselves, "For all have sinned and fall short of the glory of God" (Rom. 3:23). And, "If we say that we have no sin, we deceive ourselves, and the truth is not in us" (1 John 1:8). God tells us that if we regard iniquity in our hearts then He will not hear us. What does that mean?

Let's suppose you are like the average Christian and say, "Nobody's perfect. Everybody has some sin in his life, so this one is mine." You have a little pet sin. It may be a grudge, an attitude, or a habit. There is no repentance and sorrow for that sin but rather a regard for it.

Now let's say that you come to God to pray. And you say, "Lord, You know my child is sick, and I want You to heal my child." Do you think God's going to hear your prayer? No, He will not hear your prayer! You see it's not merely that you have sinned but that you have regard for that sin. And if He did what you were asking of Him, He would be encouraging you to sin. So He will not do what you ask.

You must deal with your sin first. You must repent of it. You must get that sin out of your heart, out of your life. And the only way to get it out is to come to the Lord and ask His forgiveness.

The Bible says in 1 John 1:9, "If we confess our sins, He is faithful and just to forgive us our sins and to cleanse us from all unrighteousness." If you are praying with unrepented sin in your heart and life, you're wasting your breath! Your prayers are not getting any higher than the lightbulbs.

Also remember that God forgives us in the manner that we forgive others. How do you forgive those who sin against you? You say, "I'm not going to forgive her." God says, "I'm not going to forgive you." Then you say, "OK, if it's that way, I'll forgive her, but I won't have any more to do with her." God says, "OK, I'll forgive you and never have any more to do with you."

Now you see, we are praying with conditions. We're saying, "Lord, You forgive me in the same manner I forgive others."

I heard about a little girl who was angry with her mother. Early one night, her mother put her to bed and told her to say her prayers before she went to sleep. The little girl got down on her knees and prayed for her brothers, sisters, daddy, aunts, uncles, and everything. Then she finished and said, "Amen." She looked up at her mother and said, "I guess you noticed you weren't in it." Well, that kind of prayer is not the kind of prayer that gets answered.

Is there unconfessed sin in your heart right now? It may be big, it may be small, but if there is sin in your life, then don't be amazed that God is not hearing your prayer. The Bible teaches in Psalm 66:18, "If I regard iniquity in my heart, the Lord will not hear."

The Protection of Prayer

Now that brings us to another important aspect of prayer—the *protection* of prayer. Matthew 6:13 says, "And do not lead us into temptation, but deliver us from the evil one." There is a devil. He is very real, and he wants to keep you from praying. He says to his demons, "Keep that person from praying because if you can keep him from praying we can beat him every time. But if he prays, he will beat us every time!"

It has been said that the devil trembles when he sees even the weakest saint upon his knees. And so, my friend, we need to pray. "Lord, lead us not into temptation."

And that brings up a real question. Does God tempt us? James 1:13 says that God tempts no man with evil. Second Peter 2:9 also says He "knows how to deliver the godly out of temptations." So this passage of the Lord's Prayer may be translated, "Lead us lest we fall into temptation." We need to pray daily that the Lord will deliver us.

Let me ask you a question. Have you ever committed a sin, asked God to forgive you, and He did? Now let me ask you another question. After you asked God to forgive you for that sin, did you commit that same sin or one like it again—even after God forgave you? And have you ever repeated that sin as many as ten times and come to God and said, "It's me again; I did it again"?

Does He continue to forgive us? If we're sincere, He does absolutely. "Seventy times seven" He will forgive you. As many times as you sin He will forgive! Praise His sweet name!

As far as God is concerned, it is the first time you ever sinned! Because He not only forgives, but He forgets our sins too! "As far as the east is from the west, so far has He removed our transgression from us" (Ps. 103:12). And in Hebrews 8:12, God tells us that He will remember our lawless deeds no more.

But wait a minute! Don't you get tired of coming back with the same old sins? Aren't you embarrassed? And aren't you ashamed that you come back and say, "Lord, it's me again. I did it again. I failed again. God have mercy on me"? Why do you keep on coming, as in Matthew 6:12, and say, "Forgive me my trespasses"? I think it is because you have understood verse 12 but you have not understood verse 13.

Verse 12 is the *pardon* of the prayer, but verse 13 is the *protection* of the prayer. And the reason we have to come back to God so many times and ask His forgiveness is that we have not put on the protection of prayer that would keep us from repeatedly falling into temptation.

Many of us jump out of bed in the morning feeling pretty good, and we do not sense any real need for prayer. The sun is shining. We have our breakfast, a cup of coffee, and sail out of the house feeling fine. And then sometime during the day the unexpected happens. We have a head-on collision with Satan. Satan digs a pit for your feet every day. He knows how to ensnare you.

The devil is not all that interested in you as a person. His real war is with God. Evil people have always known if they cannot harm someone directly, they will try to harm someone the person loves. And that is why the devil wants to harm you—so he can get at God indirectly.

And so we have become pawns in this war. The devil is the real enemy! He has made plans to sabotage us and harm our loved ones. But we go sailing through the day. Everything's fine. Then Satan tosses a bombshell in our lap. It comes so unexpectedly and we fail. At the end of the day, we say, "God I'm so sorry! Lord forgive me!" And He does.

But this is not a prayer to be prayed at the *end* of the day. This is a prayer to be prayed at the *beginning* of the day. This prayer is not the latch that closes the door at the end of the day. It is the key that opens the door at the beginning of the day.

As we wake up, we must put on the armor of our Lord Jesus Christ and make no provision for the flesh. We must immerse ourselves in the presence and power of God.

God builds a wall of fire about us as we say, "Dear Lord, deliver us from the evil one. Dear Lord, lead us lest we fall into temptation." How important that we learn how to pray!

We don't pray for protection because we think we are capable of handling it. The worst thing is not our prayerlessness; it is our pride! We think that we can go through the day and overcome the devil with our own strength. The best protection is to get off the defensive and get on the offensive.

I have a friend who was a linebacker for the Miami Dolphins. They called him Captain Crunch. He was tough and big, *and* he loved the Lord. I heard him talk about a conversation he had with his coach one day. His coach asked him, "Mike, will you do some scouting for me?" And Mike responded, "Sure, Coach, what kind of players you looking for?" The coach said, "Well, there is the player who gets knocked down and just stays there." Mike said, "We don't want him do we, Coach?" The coach said, "No!" Then the coach said, "Then there's the guy you knock down and he gets up. You knock him down again and he gets up. And you knock him down, and he just keeps getting up." Mike said, "That's the guy we want, isn't it, Coach?" The coach said, "No, we don't. I want you to find that guy that's knocking everybody down. Now that's the guy I want!"

I thank God that every time we get knocked down, He picks us up. But wouldn't you like to resist the devil and make him flee from you rather than just saying, "Lord, I'm down again, pick me up"? The Bible says in Romans 12:21, "Do not be overcome by evil, but overcome evil with good." We need to get off the defensive and on the offensive by praying, "Dear Lord, deliver me from the evil one, and lead me lest I fall into temptation."

The Praise of Prayer

Now the last thing I want you to notice is the *praise* of prayer in Matthew 6:13, "For Yours is the kingdom and the power and the glory for ever. Amen." It ends on a note of praise. And it begins on a note of praise: "Our Father in heaven, hallowed be Your name."

All powerful prayer is prayer that is packed with praise. Why? Because praise is an expression of faith! Prayer is faith turned inside out. *Faith* causes our prayers to be answered.

When we pray in the will of God with clean hearts, then we have every right to expect God to answer us. So we can begin to praise Him. And if we are having difficulty in our praying, it might be because we are not praising enough.

Billy Sunday said we need to pull some of the groans out of our prayers and shove in a few hallelujahs! Praise is a wonderful, powerful thing.

Petition goes into God's presence to carry something away. But praise goes into God's presence to stay there forever. It pleases the Lord. It blesses the Lord when we offer Him the sacrifice of praise. Powerful prayer is crammed full of praise. God inhabits the praises of His people (see Ps. 22:3).

When I got ready to go away to college, my dad said, "Son, I would like to pay your way to college; I'm not able to, but I would like to." And I said, "Dad, I appreciate the fact that you want to."

God called me to preach, and He has taken care of me. I lived from hand to mouth, and often it was God's hand to my mouth. But it meant so much to me when my dad said, "Son, I would like to if I could."

My heavenly Father will never say to me, "Son, I would like to but I can't." My heavenly Father is the King of kings. We have the heart of the Father and the hand of the King!

We have a Father who can *hear* us, and we have the King who can *answer* us. We should pray earnestly, fervently, expectantly, and praisefully unto Him.

I was talking to a young boy, and he said, "God has called me to preach, and He wants me to go to school, but I don't have any money. So I don't guess I can go." I said, "If I could get a millionaire to help you, would you go?" His eyes lit up, and he said, "I sure would." I said, "Well, you have the One who owns the world— Almighty God."

Where God *guides* He *provides*. If God can't do it, who can? God may use a millionaire, or He may use some other means, but I want to tell you that His is the kingdom, the power, and the glory! What a great God we have to pray to! And what fools we are if we do not learn how to pray.

You do not have a failure in your life except that which is really a prayer failure. There is not a sin in your life that proper prayer would not have avoided. There is not a need in your life that could not be met if you learned to pray. So I want you to say with the disciples, and with my own heart.

Lord, teach me to pray!

12

Every Christian Ought to Know

HOW TO UNDERSTAND THE BIBLE

Open my eyes, that I may see wondrous things
from Your law.

PSALM 119:18

A wise man once said, "These hath God married and no man shall part, dust on the Bible and drought in the heart." If you do not know, love, understand, practice, and obey the Word of God, I can tell you without stutter, stammer, or apology that you are not a victorious Christian.

As you read this chapter, I want you to learn how to study your Bible, how to make it burst aflame in your hand. Knowledge is power. That's true in any realm, whether it's business, athletics, or theology. I want us to look at how to obtain knowledge from the Word of God.

People today need truth. Someone in Kenya once wrote this prayer: "Lord, from the cowardice that dares not face new truth, from the laziness that is contented with half-truth, from the arrogance which thinks it has all truth, good Lord, deliver me. Amen."

I hope that you'll not have cowardice and be afraid of truth, that you'll not have laziness and accept half-truth, or that you'll not have arrogance and think that you need no truth. It is knowledge, it is truth, that transforms.

A business sign read, "We are not what we think we are; what we think, we are." Did you understand that? You are what you think. The Bible says in Proverbs 23:7, "For as he thinks in his heart, so is he."

If that is true and if knowledge is power, we need the knowledge of the Word of God to have spiritual power. We need to be molded, motivated, and managed by the Word of God. And yet for many people, the Bible remains a closed book, a mysterious book. They really do not understand it.

There is no cheap way, no lazy way, no magical way to understand the Bible. But it is not impossible. As a matter of fact, it is joyful and thrilling.

Psalm 119 is by far the longest psalm in the Bible. The writer of this psalm gives us a number of statements about the Word of God. In fact, the entire psalm, well over one hundred verses, is dealing with the Word of God, to help us know and understand the Word of God.

As you read this chapter, I want you to take note of three things. If you'll do these three things, the Bible will burst aflame in your heart, in your mind, and in your life:

- Appreciate the *virtues* of the Word of God.
- Assimilate the *vitality* of the Word of God.
- Appropriate the *values* of the Word of God.

Appreciate the Virtues of the Word of God

If you don't appreciate the virtues of the Word of God, you're not going to have any desire to learn His Word or know it. Many people do not understand the great value and virtue of the Word of God. You must appreciate the Word of God.

The Bible Is Timeless

Psalm 119:89 says, "Forever, O LORD, Your word is settled in heaven."

The Bible is not the book of the month or even the book of the year. The Bible is the book of the ages. It is an unchanging, timeless book.

Psalm 119:152 says, "Concerning Your testimonies, I have known of old that You have founded them forever."

Forever! God says that it is done. It is settled in heaven. Psalm 119:160 says, "The entirety of Your word is truth, and every one of Your righteous judgments endures forever."

Other books come and go. The Bible is here to stay. Thousands of years have passed since the Bible was written. Empires have risen and fallen. Civilizations have come and gone. Science has pushed back the frontiers of knowledge. And yet the Bible stands.

Emperors have decreed the extermination of the Bible, and atheists have railed against the Bible. Agnostics have cynically sneered at the Bible, and liberals have moved heaven and earth to remove the miracles from the Bible. Materialists have simply ignored the Bible, but the Bible stands. The Bible is settled in heaven.

The late, great Dr. Robert G. Lee had this to say about the Bible: "All of its enemies have not torn one hole in its holy vesture, nor stolen one flower from its wonderful garden, nor diluted one drop of honey from its abundant hive, nor broken one string on its thousand-stringed harp, nor drowned one sweet word in infidel ink."

Dr. Lee was simply saying what God says about Himself: "Forever, O Lord, Your word is settled in heaven" (Ps. 119:89). In the New Testament, 1 Peter 1:25 says, "But the word of the Lord endures forever."

The Bible is timeless, ultimate, indestructible.

The Bible Is Truthful

Psalm 119:142 says, "Your righteousness is an everlasting righteousness, and Your law is truth." Verse 151 says, "You are near, O Lord, and all Your commandments are truth." Then verse 160 says, "The entirety of Your word is truth."

In the Gospel of John, Pilate asked Jesus, "What is truth?" (John 18:38). Jesus had already answered that question in John 17:17 when, speaking to the Father, He said, "Your word is truth." In a world that has lost its appreciation for truth, you can say without stutter or stammer that the Bible is truth.

Today there are all kinds of attacks on the truth of the Bible. There's the frontal attack of liberals who deny the truth of the Bible. But there's also an attack from the rear, which is perhaps more insidious. These are not the people who deny the truth of the Bible. These are the people who put their own experience over the Word of God. They say, "I know what I feel or what I think." Sometimes, they'll even argue and say, "I don't care what the Bible says. Let me tell you what I experienced."

Paul had to deal with some of those people in Corinth. He said to them in 1 Corinthians 14:37–38: "If anyone thinks himself to be a prophet or spiritual, let him acknowledge that the things which I write to you are the commandments of the Lord."

Apparently some people in Corinth ventured into charismatic hocus-pocus and went wild about tongues, prophecies, visions, and ecstasies. Paul tried to set them in order, but they said, "Let me tell you, Brother Paul, what a spiritual man I am. And, let me tell you, Brother Paul, I have the gift of prophecy."

Paul says, "If you think you're a prophet or if you think you're spiritual, then you will acknowledge what I say is the Word of God." He goes on to say in verse 38, "But if anyone is ignorant, let him be ignorant."

There is the frontal attack against the truth of the Bible by those who rail against it and deny it. There's an attack from the rear by those who want to substitute their own experience for the Word of God. And there's an attack from the flank. These people don't necessarily deny the Bible. But they want to replace it or prop it up with psychology and with philosophy and other things, as if the Bible itself is not good enough.

Friend, the Bible is true, and if you're looking for truth, you can find it in the Bible.

Why? Second Timothy 3:16 says, "All scripture is given by inspiration of God." That word *inspiration* is used only once in the Bible, but what a magnificent word it is. In Greek the word is *theopneustos*. The word literally means "God-breathed." *Theo* means God. *Pneustos* means breathed. The Bible says that all Scripture is the breath of God. It is God-breathed.

In Matthew 4:4, Jesus said, "Man shall not live by bread alone, but by every word that proceeds from the mouth of God." Jesus was talking about the Bible. He said that every word proceeds from the mouth of God. It is not simply that God breathed into the Scriptures. God breathed the Scriptures out. Yes, He used men such as Isaiah, Jeremiah, Matthew, Mark, and Paul. But these men held the pen of God. They were the voice of God as God was speaking. The Bible is true because the God of truth cannot speak error.

If you read the Old Testament, you will find phrases like "the Word of the Lord" or "the Word of God" or "God spoke" or "the Lord said" used 3,808 times. If the Bible is not the Word of God, it's the biggest bundle of lies that has ever come to planet Earth. The Bible is truth, absolutely.

The Bible Is Treasured

Because the Bible is a *timeless* book and a *truthful* book, it should therefore be a *treasured* book. In Psalm 119:72, the psalmist says, "The law of Your mouth is better to me than thousands of coins of gold and silver."

Is that true of you? God knows that it is absolutely true of me. If you were to ask me to choose between a huge stack of gold, silver, rubies, diamonds, stocks, and bonds on the one hand, or the Word of God on the other, I would not hesitate. I would choose the Word of God. Psalm 119:103 says, "How sweet are Your words to my taste, sweeter than honey to my mouth!" Verse 127 says,

"Therefore I love Your commandments more than gold, yes, than fine gold."

The Bible is to be a treasured book. The saints and the heroes of our faith have pillowed their heads on the Word of God as they walked through the chilly waters of the river of death. The martyrs who died for the witness of Jesus Christ have held the Bible to their bosoms as the creeping flames came around their feet. The members of the early church loved the Word of God. They never questioned it, and they argued little about it. They preached it, proclaimed it, pronounced it, and poured it forth like white-hot lava. They loved it, lived it, practiced it, trusted it, and obeyed it. They claimed it constantly.

Do you know why the Bible is treasured? You've known it for a long time. "Jesus loves me, this I know, for the Bible tells me so." That's it. "Jesus loves me, this I know, for the Bible tells me so." You will never have a victorious Christian life if you do not love this book.

The Bible is like treasure. Suppose there was buried treasure in your backyard. You'd go down to the hardware store and get a spade if you didn't already have one. The Bible is God's treasure book. It is a timeless book. It is a truthful book. Therefore, you must appreciate the virtues of the Word of God. If you don't appreciate the virtues of the Word of God, you're not going to have any desire to understand it.

Assimilate the Vitality of the Word of God

The word *vitality* means "alive." The Bible is a *living* book. Hebrews 4:12 says, "For the word of God is living and powerful."

235

The word *"powerful"* comes from the Greek word *energes* which means "effective." This is the word from which we get our word *energy*. The Bible is alive. It is effective.

In John 6:63, Jesus spoke to a group of unbelievers and His disciples saying, "The words that I speak to you are spirit, and they are life." The Bible pulsates with life. For instance, you don't just read a cookbook. You use its instructions to prepare a meal, then you eat it. If you don't assimilate it, no matter how much you appreciate it, what good is it going to do you?

Pray over the Word of God

How do you assimilate the Word of God? Pray over it. Psalm 119:12 says, "Blessed are You, O LORD! Teach me Your statutes." Have you ever prayed that? "Lord God, be my Teacher." Pray over the Word of God and ask God to teach you.

First, *your eyes will be opened.* Read in Psalm 119:18: "Open my eyes, that I may see wondrous things from Your law." God will open your eyes. You may have 20/20 vision, but God has to open your eyes in order for you to behold the wondrous things in His Word.

After His resurrection, Jesus walked with two disciples on the road to Emmaus. The Bible says that He began to talk to them about the Old Testament, the Law, and the Prophets. Then, Luke 24:45 says, "And He opened their understanding, that they might comprehend the Scriptures." Wouldn't you like God to do that for you?

When you pray over the Word of God, not only will your eyes be opened, but *your heart will be stirred.* Psalm 119:36 says, "Incline my heart to Your testimonies, and not to covetousness." If you don't have a desire for the Word of God, then pray, "Oh God, please incline my heart. Move my heart, open my eyes, stir my heart."

And then, when your eyes are opened and your heart is stirred, *your mind is going to be enlightened.* Psalm 119:73 says, "Your hands have made me and fashioned me; give me understanding, that I may learn Your commandments."

How often in sermon preparation have I put down my pencil and bowed my head to say, "Oh my God, help me to understand this. God, give me understanding." When we pray, our eyes are opened, our hearts are moved, and our minds are enlightened to understand the Word of God.

Ponder the Word of God

Psalm 119:15 says, "I will meditate on Your precepts." Verse 147 of this psalm says, "I rise before the dawning of the morning, and cry for help; I hope in Your word." In other words, he had a quiet time. The psalmist continues in verse 148: "My eyes are awake through the night watches, that I may meditate on Your word."

It takes time to ponder the Word of God. If you have to rise an hour early, do it. If you have to stay up an hour late, do it. Do whatever it takes so that you might ponder the Word of God. And may I suggest that as you ponder the Word of God, you keep a pad and pencil handy? I always read the Bible with a pen or a pencil in my hand. Why? Because I'm *expecting to receive something.* If you're not doing that, it tells me that you're not expecting to receive anything.

If you're expecting to receive something, you should be ready to write it down. You say, "I'll remember it." I hope you do. But the weakest ink is better than the best memory. It's such a simple thing to get a pad and pencil when you open the Bible. You pray over it, you ponder it, and then you get ready for God to speak to you.

And when you read the Bible, use your sanctified common sense. Don't just jump into the middle of a chapter or the middle of a book somewhere with no plan. The Bible is like any other book in that it contains a number of different forms of speech. You see poetry as poetry. You see prophecy as prophecy. You see precept as precept. You see promise as promise. You see proverb as proverb.

If you try to turn the proverbs into promises, you'll lose your religion. The proverbs are not promises. They're proverbs. What is a proverb? A proverb is a general principle that when generally applied brings a general result.

For example, the book of Proverbs has ways to be healthy, wealthy, and wise. But you can do all those things and get hit by a truck. You're not very healthy anymore. And you're certainly not wealthy; you left it all. If you'd been wise, you would've looked both ways. The proverbs are good, but don't try to turn the proverbs into promises.

Look at the Bible and consider what you are reading. Ask yourself, "Is this a precept? Is this a prophecy? Is this poetry? Is this prose? Is this proverb? Is this promise?" God gave you a mind. But God doesn't zap you with knowledge. You have the mind of Christ. Use your mind. As you study the Bible, you should ponder it.

Sometimes people ask, "Is the Bible to be interpreted literally or figuratively?" The answer is, "Yes." The Bible is to be interpreted figuratively *and* literally all at the same time.

The Bible, for example, is full of symbols. In the book of Revelation, the devil is symbolized as a huge dragon. He has a tail so long that he sweeps a third of the stars from heaven.

Today technology allows us to look billions of light-years into outer space. Now, you tell me if there's a dragon with a tail long enough to sweep down all the stars of heaven some billions of light-years away. That's a pretty big dragon. This passage is talking about the devil. The stars are the fallen angels that fell. That is symbolism.

Let me give you an example from everyday life. When you're driving down the highway and you see the yellow arches, you know that you're approaching a McDonald's. When you see those yellow arches, do you say, "Oh, that's just a symbol. There is no McDonald's restaurant, and there is no such thing as a hamburger"? Of course not. The arches are a symbol of a reality. You find out what the symbol stands for, and then you literally apply it.

When you get the Word of God, pray over it, ponder it, and then ask God to teach you. Here are six age-old questions to ask when studying the Word of God.

1. Is there a promise to claim?
2. Is there a lesson to learn?
3. Is there a blessing to enjoy?
4. Is there a command to obey?
5. Is there a sin to avoid?
6. Is there a new thought to carry with me?

These are great starter questions when preparing a Sunday school lesson or a Bible study. You can take any passage of Scripture and ask those questions and you've got your lesson! I promise you. Just ask these six simple questions as you study the Word of God, and God will give you the lesson He wants you to learn.

Preserve the Word of God

After you pray and ponder over the Word of God, then you preserve the Word of God. Psalm 119:11 says, "Your word I have hidden in my heart, that I might not sin against You." Verse 16 of that same psalm says, "I will delight myself in Your statutes; I will not forget Your word."

That means that you hide the Word of God in your heart. You can remember far more than you think you can remember. In fact, we function by memory. Memory comes with concentration, motivation, and use. Your mind is a marvel, and you can remember far more than you think you can remember as you preserve the Word of God.

My wife enjoys collecting pretty little boxes. Sometimes people will bring her boxes from other countries. They may be intricately carved or covered in jewels. You see one and say, "What a marvelous little box." Then you open it up to look inside. Do you know what's inside that beautiful little box? It contains things like rubber bands, paper clips, toothpicks, or an old breath mint. Your mind is like that box. God gave you a marvelous mind, and you've got all this junk in it.

Your mind can also be compared to a garden. Have you ever noticed how much easier it is to grow weeds than flowers and vegetables? When Adam fell, his mind became a garden of weeds. In order for your mind to preserve the Word of God, you have to cultivate your mind. You have to weed your garden. Fill your mind with the Word of God so what is inside will flow forth blessing and honor to God.

Practice the Word of God

Psalm 119:1–5 says, "Blessed are the undefiled in the way, who walk in the law of the LORD! Blessed are those who keep His testimonies, who seek Him with the whole heart! They also do no iniquity; they walk in His ways. You have commanded us to keep Your precepts diligently. Oh, that my ways were directed to keep Your statutes!"

It's not enough to *recite* the promises without *obeying* the commandments. Do you want to learn more about the Word of God? Then obey the part you already know. That is so simple. The Bible says, "For whoever has, to him more will be given, and he will have abundance" (Matt. 13:12).

The more you obey, the more you will learn. You might be saying to yourself, "There's a lot of the Bible I don't understand." Do you know what Mark Twain is reported to have said? "It's not that part of the Bible I don't understand that gives me so much trouble. It's the part I do understand." Keep the Word of God!

There may be mysteries and things you don't understand like the third toe on the left foot of a beast in Revelation. But I will tell you one thing you *can* understand, "Love one another." You can understand when the Bible gives you clear and plain commandments. And, if you will begin to keep the things that you *do* understand, the Word of God will become real to you.

Proclaim the Word of God

Psalm 119:13 says, "With my lips I have declared all the judgments of Your mouth." Look at verse 27: "Make me understand the way of Your precepts; so shall I meditate on Your wonderful works." Then, in verse 46: "I will speak of Your testimonies also before kings, and will not be ashamed." Finally, look at verse 172: "My tongue shall speak of Your word, for all Your commandments are righteousness."

Let the Word of God be constantly in your mouth. Stow it in your heart, show it in your life, sow it in the world. The more of the Word of God you give away, the more of it will stick to you.

Appropriate the Values of the Word of God

You must *appreciate the virtues* of the Word of God, *assimilate the vitality* of the Word of God, *appropriate the values* of the Word of God. When you do that, this knowledge will transform your life.

A Source of Victory

Psalm 119:45 says, "And I will walk at liberty, for I seek Your precepts." Just as Jesus appropriated the Word of God to overcome Satan in the wilderness, so you can overcome. The Word of God can become your source of victory.

A Source of Growth

Psalm 119:32 says, "I will run the course of Your commandments, for You shall enlarge my heart."

A person might come to me and say, "I'm just so weak in my physical life. I can hardly get out of bed. I just don't want to go to work. I'm just so weak."

Then I might say, "What's the matter? Have you been to the doctor?"

"No," he says.

"Have you got a disease?"

"I don't think so," he says.

"What are you eating?"

"I have this restaurant I go to on Sundays sometimes if it's not raining, and I get a meal there. That's all I eat," he says.

"You mean that's all you eat? You just go to this restaurant on Sunday, and you get a meal there if it's not raining? And that's all you eat?"

"Yeah, I'm just so weak."

Well, of course he's weak.

Friend, a sermon on Sunday is designed just to whet your appetite. If you don't learn how to feed yourself the Word of God, you're not going to grow. The Bible says, "As newborn babes, desire the pure milk of the word, that you may grow thereby" (1 Pet. 2:2). The Word of God is your source of growth.

A Source of Joy

Psalm 119:54 says, "Your statutes have been my songs in the house of my pilgrimage."

Verse 111 of this psalm says, "Your testimonies I have taken as a heritage forever, for they are the rejoicing of my heart."

In John 15:11, Jesus said, "These things I have spoken to you, that My joy may remain in you, and that your joy may be full." The Word of God is a source of joy.

A Source of Power

The Word of God is your power source for victorious living. "For the word of God is living and powerful" (Heb. 4:12).

Psalm 119:28 says, "My soul melts from heaviness; strengthen me according to Your word." The Bible is our source of power.

A Source of Guidance

Psalm 119:105 says, "Your word is a lamp to my feet and a light to my path." We can find our way when we study and meditate upon His Word. It may be dark, but His Word will show us the way if we trust Him.

Do you want victory? Do you want growth? Do you want joy? Do you want power? Do you want guidance? Friend, the Word of

God will give you all of these things. You can appropriate them. But you can only appropriate them after you assimilate them. And you can only assimilate them if you appreciate them. I promise you that if you'll do these things, the Word of God will transform your life.

IT'S NOT HOW MUCH YOU KNOW, IT'S HOW MUCH YOU *GROW*

"Knowledge puffs up, but love edifies" (1 Cor. 8:1).

I opened this book with the proposition that what you don't know *can* hurt you. Unfortunately, for some, knowledge and doctrine become an end in themselves.

The ultimate yardstick of your life as a believer is not how much you know but how much you *grow*. The purpose of this book has not been primarily information or inspiration but transformation.

Paul tells the aim of his ministry to the church at Ephesus.

... till we all come to the unity of the faith and of the knowledge of the Son of God, to a perfect man, to the measure of the stature of the fullness of Christ; that we should no longer be children, tossed to and fro and carried about wth every wind of doctrine, by the trickery of men, in the cunning craftiness of deceitful plotting, but, speaking the truth in love, may grow up in all things into Him who is the head—Christ—from whom the whole body, joined and knit together by what every joint supplies, according to the effective working by

which every part does its share, causes growth of the
body for the edifying of itself in love. (Eph. 4:13–16)

In this passage Paul was telling the saints to grow up.

We Are to Be Mature in Stature

". . . till we all come to the unity of the faith and of the knowledge of the Son of God, to a perfect man, to the measure of the
stature of the fullness of Christ" (Eph. 4:13).

When I was a kid, my parents let us stand against a wall in the
house. A mark was then placed on the wall that measured our
height. From time to time, we would stand with our backs straight
against that wall to see if we were growing. I remember stretching
myself as tall as I could. Then my parents would measure my growth
with the yardstick.

God measures His children with a different standard, "the
measure of the stature of the fullness of Christ."

The standard and goal of your maturity is that you are to be like
the Lord Jesus Christ. As a kid, I would measure my growth against
that of my brother. It is time that we as Christians quit comparing
ourselves with others and measure ourselves by Him. We may look
fairly good if we compare ourselves with others, but Jesus is the standard. Are you becoming more and more like the Him?

We Are to Be Mature in Stability

". . . that we should no longer be children, tossed to and fro and
carried about with every wind of doctrine, by the trickery of men, in
the cunning craftiness of deceitful plotting" (Eph. 4:14).

There are those who by cunning craftiness are ready to lead the immature Christian astray. It is heartbreaking to see many immature Christians who are led into false cults and bizarre beliefs. I used to be amazed that some would not believe. After many years, I am now even more amazed at what some will believe.

G. K. Chesterson is reported to have said, "When men stop believing in God, it is not that they then believe in nothing. Rather, it is that they will believe in anything." I might add that if Christians are not firmly rooted and growing, they too are apt to believe almost anything. They are "sitting ducks" for Satan's big guns.

The average pastor is heartsick over immature Christians who are lost, strayed or stolen. Genuine truth ought to help you to be a steadfast Christian.

We Are to be Mature in Speech

". . . but, speaking the truth in love, may grow up in all things into Him who is the head—Christ" (Eph. 4:15).

Why are there so many in the church with hurt feelings? And why is there so much division in modern Christianity? One of the chief reasons is immature Christians who act like children in their speech. Of course, we must speak the truth. That is a given. That's why we have written *What Every Christian Ought to Know*. But we need more than Bible truth. We need love that comes with Christian growth and maturity.

There need be no division between truth and love. Some have made that division. Truth without love may be a form of brutality. Love without truth may be empty sentimentality. May God deliver us from the immature pronouncements of those who have loveless truth and the immature emotionalism of those who have truthless love.

With truth and no love one may swell up. With love and no truth one may blow up. But truth and love cause the Christian to grow up.

We Are to Be Mature in Service

". . . from whom the whole body, joined and knit together by what every joint supplies, according to the effective working by which every part does its share, causes growth of the body for the edifying of itself in love" (Eph. 4:16).

Each part in a healthy body helps the other parts, each in its own way. By love we serve one another.

This verse speaks of the church as a body and mentions joints. The Greek word for joint is *harmos*. We get our word *harmony* from this word. Mature people work together in harmonious interaction like the joints in a body. Mature people can work together if the joints of the body (the church) are lubricated with love. This comes with maturity.

A cathedral in England was destroyed by German bombs during World War II. Some students helped to rebuild it. A statue of Jesus in the cathedral had been damaged. The students pieced it together, but the hands had been destroyed beyond retrieval. Rather than replace the hands, they placed a plaque beneath the statue that read, "Christ has no hands but ours." There is a great truth to that. May God help you to find a place of service and let your hands be His hands.

As we bring all of this to a conclusion, remember that you are to grow with what you have learned. Keep growing! Remember that when you cease to be better, you will cease to be good.

ENDNOTES

Chapter 1, "Every Christian Ought to Know the Bible Is the Word of God"

1. W. A. Criswell, *The Bible for Today's World* (Grand Rapids: Zondervan, 1965), 17.

2. Ibid., 17.

3. William Wilson gives these meanings for the Hebrew *chuwg*: "circle, sphere, the arch or vault of the heavens; the circle of the earth, *orbis terrarium*." William Wilson, *New Wilson's Old Testament Word Studies* (Grand Rapids: Kregel, 1987).

4. S. I. McMillen, *None of These Diseases* (Grand Rapids: Fleming H. Revell Co., 2001).

Chapter 2, "Every Christian Ought to Know the Assurance of Salvation"

1. "That He might sanctify and cleanse her with the washing of water by the word" (Eph. 5:26). "Having been born again, not of corruptible seed but incorruptible, through the word of God which lives and abides forever" (1 Pet. 1:23).

Chapter 4, "Every Christian Ought to Know What Happens When a Christian Sins"

1. "Come Thou Fount Of Every Blessing," lyrics by Robert Robinson, 1758.
2. Augustus Toplady, "Rock of Ages," 1775.

Chapter 5, "Every Christian Ought to Know How to Handle Temptation"

1. C. C. Mitchell, *Let's Live* (Grand Rapids: Revell, 1975).
2. Helen Lemmel, "Turn Your Eyes upon Jesus," 1922.

Chapter 6, "Every Christian Ought to Know about Believers Baptism"

1. *Constitutions of the Holy Apostles,* Book 3, Section 16/17.
2. *Hippolytus—Creeds of the Church,* Ages Software, 7.
3. John Calvin, *Institutes,* chapter 15.
4. *History of the Apostolic Church,* 568.
5. *Faith of Our Fathers,* 275.
6. W. E. Vines in his *Expository Dictionary of New Testament Words* defines *baptizō* as "to baptize, a frequentative form of *baptō,* to dip."

Chapter 9, "Every Christian Ought to Know How to Be Filled with the Holy Spirit"

1. George Atkins, "Brethren, We Have Met to Worship," 1819.